M

MARY

Grace and Hope in Christ

The Seattle Statement of the Anglican–Roman Catholic
International Commission
The Text with Commentaries and Study Guide

Edited by Donald Bolen
and Gregory Cameron

continuum

Continuum

The Tower Building, 11 York Road, London SE1 7NX

80 Maiden Lane, Suite 704, New York, NY 10038, USA

Published by Continuum for the Anglican Consultative Council, London, and the Pontifical Council for Promoting Christian Unity, Rome

Unless otherwise indicated, biblical quotations are from the New Revised Standard Version Bible, copyright 1989, Division of Christian Education of the National Council of the Churches of Christ in the United States of America. Used by permission. All rights reserved.

Cover art: Basilica di Santa Maria Sopra Minerva, Rome
Camera di Santa Caterina da Siena
The Annunciation
Photo: PP Domenicani
By the kind courtesy of the Department for Monuments and Artistic Treasures, Italy

Artwork by Steve Erspamer from *Religious Clip Art for the Liturgical Year (A, B, and C)*. Used by permission of Liturgy Training Publications.

Back cover art: Mary and Child
Anglican Church of St Gregory and St Martin, Wye, Kent
Photo: Jim Rosenthal, Anglican Episcopal World

British Library Cataloguing-in-Publication Data
A catalogue record for this book is available from the British Library

ISBN 0–8264–8155–8

Printed and bound in England by Antony Rowe Ltd, Chippenham, Wiltshire

✤ Contents

✤
Introduction

This is a book in seven parts.

At the heart of the book is the text of the Agreed Statement by the Anglican–Roman Catholic International Commission, *Mary: Grace and Hope in Christ* (referred to in this text as 'the Mary statement' or MGHC), which was published in May 2005 as the culmination of a process of five years of study and reflection by the Commission. It is not an official statement of the Anglican Communion or the Catholic Church, but it does represent the sustained thinking of significant Roman Catholic and Anglican theologians as they studied together an important aspect of Christian faith down through the centuries. The statement registers a large measure of agreement between them on the place and understanding of Mary in Christian faith and devotion, and it has been published for consideration and assessment by the churches of the Anglican Communion and the Catholic Church.

Supporting the Mary text are four significant commentaries

—two Anglican and two Roman Catholic. First are the two commentaries officially commissioned and published by the Anglican Communion Office or the Pontifical Council for Promoting Christian Unity to accompany the Agreed Statement and to introduce it to the members of the Anglican Communion and the Catholic Church. These commentaries, by Dr Timothy Bradshaw, an Anglican theologian teaching in Oxford University in England, and Fr Jared Wicks S. J., former Dean of Theology at the Gregorian University in Rome, are useful analyses of the document, asking how its fresh statement of the teaching of the Christian Church on Mary measures up to official teaching or understanding in the two Communions.

Also included in this volume are two commentaries specially commissioned for this work—two essays by members of the Commission—one Anglican, one Roman Catholic—looking into the method of the Commission's work: how did Anglican and Catholic theologians come to the conclusions which they did? What were the theological points which each side felt needed to be addressed from the perspective of their churches? What assured them that they could sign the Agreed Statement as an adequate expression of shared understanding? Sr Sara Butler MSBT, Professor of Dogmatic Theology of St Joseph's Seminary, New

York, tells the story from the Roman Catholic side, Dr Charles Sherlock, Director of Ministry Studies of the Melbourne College of Divinity, from the Anglican.

Another major component of the book is the Study Guide to accompany the Mary statement. Drawing out the key themes in the Anglican-Roman Catholic International Commission (ARCIC) text, this guide is intended for use in parishes and ecumenical study groups, where there may be no particular training or grounding in theology. It is designed to help the ordinary worshipper in Anglican or Catholic churches to understand more deeply the extraordinary riches that Christians have discovered through the ages when they have allowed Mary to become a focus of their thoughts or Christian devotion — not as a replacement for Christ, the incarnate Son of God and redeemer of the world, but as someone who points to her son, and says: "Do whatever he tells you" (John 2:5).

The authors, who are the Anglican and Catholic Secretaries of ARCIC, hope that this study will introduce the Agreed Statement to many who might otherwise think that it is intended strictly for scholars. It was certainly ARCIC's hope that the document would be an instrument through which Anglicans and Roman Catholics could come together in ecumenical encounter, and a means of strengthening and encouraging their Christian faith and understanding. The study has been designed for use by groups over a six week period—perhaps weekly gatherings during Lent or the traditional month for Catholic devotion to Mary, May—but could be used by individuals who wish to find out more about Mary and the work that ARCIC has done in considering her place and role in Christian faith today.

Finally, a seventh thread of the document is presented in the illustrations. Throughout the centuries Mary has been depicted in the iconography of religious devotion. These images have helped to make her accessible in the meditations and worship of countless Christians, and several key examples have been selected by Canon Jim Rosenthal, Director of Communications at the Anglican Communion Office, to complement the text.

We would also like to acknowledge the assistance of the Revd Terrie Robinson of the Department of Ecumenical Affairs at the Anglican Communion Office, and Ms Giovanni Ramon of the Pontifical Council for Promoting Christian Unity for their work and help in proofreading these texts and preparing them for publication.

We hope that you will enjoy this book: that it will be of use in parishes, academic institutions, and indeed, any context where Anglican and Roman Catholic believers, or other Christians, are interested in reflecting upon the mother of Our Lord. May it help to deepen our faith, extend our understanding and stimulate Christians to join together to praise God, who "has done great things".

Donald Bolen

Gregory K. Cameron

November 2005

The Seattle Statement

*Preface by the
Co-Chairmen*

In the continuing journey toward full communion, the Roman Catholic Church and the Churches of the Anglican Communion have for many years prayerfully considered a number of questions concerning the faith we share and the way we articulate it in the life and worship of our two households of faith. We have submitted Agreed Statements to the Holy See and to the Anglican Communion for comment, further clarification if necessary, and conjoint acceptance as congruent with the faith of Anglicans and Roman Catholics.

In framing this Agreed Statement, we have drawn on the Scriptures and the common tradition which predates the Reformation and the Counter Reformation. As in previous Anglican-Roman Catholic International

Commission (ARCIC) documents, we have attempted to use language that reflects what we hold in common and transcends the controversies of the past. At the same time, in this statement we have had to face squarely dogmatic definitions which are integral to the faith of Roman Catholics but largely foreign to the faith of Anglicans. The members of ARCIC, over time, have sought to embrace one another's ways of doing theology and have considered together the historical context in which certain doctrines developed. In so doing, we have learned to receive anew our own traditions, illumined and deepened by the understanding of and appreciation for each other's tradition.

Our Agreed Statement concerning the Blessed Virgin Mary as pattern of grace and hope is a powerful reflection of our efforts to seek out what we hold in common and celebrates important aspects of our common heritage. Mary, the mother of our Lord Jesus Christ, stands before us as an exemplar of faithful obedience, and her "Be it to me according to your word" is the grace-filled response each of us is called to make to God, both personally and communally, as the Church, the body of Christ. It is as figure of the Church, her arms uplifted in prayer and praise, her hands open in receptivity and availability to the outpouring of the Holy Spirit, that we are one with Mary as she magnifies the Lord. "Surely", Mary declares in her song recorded in the Gospel of Luke, "from this day all generations will call me blessed."

Our two traditions share many of the same feasts associated with Mary. From our experience we have found that it is in the realm of worship that we realize our deepest convergence as we give thanks to God for the Mother of the Lord who is one with us in that vast community of love and prayer we call the communion of saints.

✠ Alexander J. Brunett

✠ Peter F. Carnley

Seattle

Feast of the Presentation

2 February 2004

The Status of
the Document

The document published here is the work of the Anglican–Roman Catholic International Commission (ARCIC). It is a joint statement of the Commission. The authorities who appointed the Commission have allowed the statement to be published so that it may be widely discussed. It is not an authoritative declaration by the Roman Catholic Church or by the Anglican Communion, who will study and evaluate the document in due course.

Citations from Scripture are normally taken from the New Revised Standard Version. In some cases the Commission has offered its own translation.

The Seattle Statement

Mary: Grace and Hope in Christ

INTRODUCTION

1   In honouring Mary as Mother of the Lord, all gen-
    erations of Anglicans and Roman Catholics have
    echoed the greeting of Elizabeth: "Blessed are you
    among women, and blessed is the fruit of your
    womb" (Luke 1:42). The Anglican–Roman Catholic
    International Commission now offers this Agreed
    Statement on the place of Mary in the life and doc-
    trine of the Church in the hope that it expresses our
    common faith about the one who, of all believers, is
    closest to our Lord and Saviour Jesus Christ. We do
    so at the request of our two Communions, in response
    to questions set before us. A special consultation of

Anglican and Roman Catholic bishops, meeting under the leadership of the Archbishop of Canterbury, Dr George Carey, and Cardinal Edward I Cassidy, President of the Pontifical Council for Promoting Christian Unity at Mississauga, Canada, in 2000, specifically asked ARCIC for "a study of Mary in the life and doctrine of the Church". This request recalls the observation of the Malta Report (1968) that "real or apparent differences between us come to the surface in such matters as . . . the Mariological definitions" promulgated in 1854 and 1950. More recently, in *Ut Unum Sint* (1995), Pope John Paul II identified as one area in need of fuller study by all Christian traditions before a true consensus of faith can be achieved "the Virgin Mary, as Mother of God and Icon of the Church, the spiritual Mother who intercedes for Christ's disciples and for all humanity" (para. 79).

2 ARCIC has addressed this topic once before. *Authority in the Church II* (1981) already records a significant degree of agreement:

> We agree that there can be but one mediator between God and man, Jesus Christ, and reject any interpretation of the role of Mary which

obscures this affirmation. We agree in recognizing that Christian understanding of Mary is inseparably linked with the doctrines of Christ and the Church. We agree in recognising the grace and unique vocation of Mary, Mother of God Incarnate (*Theotókos*), in observing her festivals, and in according her honour in the communion of saints. We agree that she was prepared by divine grace to be the mother of our Redeemer, by whom she herself was redeemed and received into glory. We further agree in recognising in Mary a model of holiness, obedience, and faith for all Christians. We accept that it is possible to regard her as a prophetic figure of the Church of God before as well as after the Incarnation (para. 30).

The same document, however, points out remaining differences:

The dogmas of the Immaculate Conception and the Assumption raise a special problem for those Anglicans who do not consider that the precise definitions given by these dogmas are sufficiently supported by Scripture. For many Anglicans the teaching authority of the bishop

of Rome, independent of a council, is not recommended by the fact that through it these
Marian doctrines were proclaimed as dogmas
binding on all the faithful. Anglicans would also
ask whether, in any future union between our
two Churches, they would be required to sub-
scribe to such dogmatic statements (para. 30).

These reservations in particular were noted in the
official *Response of the Holy See to The Final Report*
(1991, para. 13). Having taken these shared beliefs
and these questions as the starting point for our
reflection, we are now able to affirm further significant agreement on the place of Mary in the life and
doctrine of the Church.

3 The present document proposes a fuller statement of
our shared belief concerning the Blessed Virgin
Mary and so provides the context for a common
appreciation of the content of the Marian dogmas.
We also take up differences of practice, including the
explicit invocation of Mary. This new study of Mary
has benefited from our previous study of reception in
The Gift of Authority (1999). There we concluded that,
when the Church receives and acknowledges what it
recognizes as a true expression of the Tradition once

for all delivered to the Apostles, this reception is an act both of faithfulness and of freedom. The freedom to respond in fresh ways in the face of new challenges is what enables the Church to be faithful to the Tradition which it carries forward. At other times, some element of the apostolic Tradition may be forgotten, neglected, or abused. In such situations, fresh recourse to Scripture and Tradition recalls God's revelation in Christ: we call this process *re-reception* (cf. *Gift* 24–5). Progress in ecumenical dialogue and understanding suggests that we now have an opportunity to re-receive together the tradition of Mary's place in God's revelation.

4 Since its inception ARCIC has sought to get behind opposed or entrenched positions to discover and develop our common inheritance of faith (cf. *Authority I*, 25). Following *The Common Declaration* in 1966 of Pope Paul VI and the Archbishop of Canterbury, Dr Michael Ramsey, we have continued our "serious dialogue . . . founded on the Gospels and on the ancient common traditions." We have asked to what extent doctrine or devotion concerning Mary belongs to a legitimate 'reception' of the apostolic Tradition, in accordance with the Scriptures. This Tradition has at its core the proclamation of the trinitarian 'economy

of salvation'. grounding the life and faith of the Church in the divine communion of Father, Son, and Spirit. We have sought to understand Mary's person and role in the history of salvation and the life of the Church in the light of a theology of divine grace and hope. Such a theology is deeply rooted in the enduring experience of Christian worship and devotion.

5 God's grace calls for and enables human response (cf. *Salvation and the Church*, 9). This is seen in the Gospel account of the Annunciation, where the angel's message evokes the response of Mary. The Incarnation and all that it entailed, including the passion, death, and resurrection of Christ and the birth of the Church, came about by way of Mary's freely uttered *fiat*—"let it be done to me according to your word" (Luke 1:38). We recognize in the event of the Incarnation God's gracious 'Yes' to humanity as a whole. This reminds us once more of the Apostle's words in 2 Corinthians 1:18–20 (*Gift* 8ff): all God's promises find their 'Yes' in the Son of God, Jesus Christ. In this context, Mary's *fiat* can be seen as the supreme instance of a believer's 'Amen' in response to the 'Yes' of God. Christian disciples respond to the same 'Yes' with their own 'Amen.' They thus know themselves to be children together of the one heavenly

Father, born of the Spirit as brothers and sisters of Jesus Christ, drawn into the communion of love of the blessed Trinity. Mary epitomizes such participation in the life of God. Her response was not made without profound questioning, and it issued in a life of joy intermingled with sorrow, taking her even to the foot of her son's cross. When Christians join in Mary's 'Amen' to the 'Yes' of God in Christ, they commit themselves to an obedient response to the Word of God, which leads to a life of prayer and service. Like Mary, they not only magnify the Lord with their lips: they commit themselves to serve God's justice with their lives (cf. Luke 1:46–55).

A MARY ACCORDING TO THE SCRIPTURES

6 We remain convinced that the holy Scriptures, as the Word of God written, bear normative witness to God's plan of salvation, so it is to them that this statement first turns. Indeed, it is impossible to be faithful to Scripture and not to take Mary seriously. We recognize, however, that for some centuries Anglicans and Roman Catholics have interpreted the Scriptures while divided from one another. In reflecting together on the Scriptures' testimony concerning Mary, we have discovered more than just a few tantalizing

glimpses into the life of a great saint. We have found ourselves meditating with wonder and gratitude on the whole sweep of salvation history: creation, election, the Incarnation, passion, and resurrection of Christ, the gift of the Spirit in the Church, and the final vision of eternal life for all God's people in the new creation.

7   In the following paragraphs, our use of Scripture seeks to draw upon the whole tradition of the Church, in which rich and varied readings have been employed. In the New Testament, the Old Testament is commonly interpreted typologically[1]: events and images are understood with specific reference to Christ. This approach is further developed by the Fathers and by medieval preachers and authors. The Reformers stressed the clarity and sufficiency of Scripture, and called for a return to the centrality of the Gospel message. Historical-critical approaches

---

1. By typology we mean a reading which accepts that certain things in Scripture (persons, places, and events) foreshadow or illuminate other things, or reflect patterns of faith in imaginative ways (e.g. Adam is a type of Christ: Romans 5:14; Isaiah 7:14 points towards the virgin birth of Jesus: Matthew 1:23). This typological sense was considered to be a meaning that goes beyond the literal sense. This approach assumes the unity and consistency of the divine revelation.

attempted to discern the meaning intended by the biblical authors, and to account for texts' origins. Each of these readings has its limitations, and may give rise to exaggerations or imbalances: typology can become extravagant, Reformation emphases reductionist, and critical methods overly historicist. More recent approaches to Scripture point to the range of possible readings of a text, notably its narrative, rhetorical, and sociological dimensions. In this statement, we seek to integrate what is valuable from each of these approaches, as both correcting and contributing to our use of Scripture. Further, we recognize that no reading of a text is neutral, but each is shaped by the context and interest of its readers. Our reading has taken place within the context of our dialogue in Christ, for the sake of that communion which is his will. It is thus an ecclesial and ecumenical reading, seeking to consider each passage about Mary in the context of the New Testament as a whole, against the background of the Old, and in the light of Tradition.

The Witness of Scripture: A Trajectory of Grace and Hope

8 The Old Testament bears witness to God's creation of men and women in the divine image, and God's

loving call to covenant relationship with himself. Even when they disobeyed, God did not abandon human beings to sin and the power of death. Again and again God offered a covenant of grace. God made a covenant with Noah that never again would "all flesh" be destroyed by the waters of a flood. The Lord made a covenant with Abraham that, through him, all the families of the earth might be blessed. Through Moses he made a covenant with Israel that, obedient to his word, they might be a holy nation and a priestly people. The prophets repeatedly summoned the people to turn back from disobedience to the gracious God of the covenant, to receive God's word and let it bear fruit in their lives. They looked forward to a renewal of the covenant in which there would be perfect obedience and perfect self-giving: "This is the covenant that I will make with the house of Israel after those days, says the LORD: I will put my law within them, and I will write it on their hearts; and I will be their God, and they shall be my people" (Jeremiah 31:33). In the prophecy of Ezekiel, this hope is spoken of not only in terms of washing and cleansing, but also of the gift of the Spirit (Ezekiel 36:25–8).

9 The covenant between the Lord and his people is several times described as a love affair between God

and Israel, the virgin daughter of Zion, bride and mother: "I gave you my solemn oath and entered into a covenant with you, declares the Sovereign Lord, and you became mine" (Ezekiel 16:8; cf. Isaiah 54:1 and Galatians 4:27). Even in punishing faithlessness, God remains forever faithful, promising to restore the covenant relationship and to draw together the scattered people (Hosea 1–2; Jeremiah 2:2, 31:3; Isaiah 62:4–5). Nuptial imagery is also used within the New Testament to describe the relationship between Christ and the Church (Ephesians 5:21–33; Revelation 21:9). In parallel to the prophetic image of Israel as the bride of the Lord, the Solomonic literature of the Old Testament characterizes Holy Wisdom as the handmaid of the Lord (Proverbs 8.22f; cf. Wisdom 7:22–6) similarly emphasizing the theme of responsiveness and creative activity. In the New Testament these prophetic and wisdom motifs are combined (Luke 11:49) and fulfilled in the coming of Christ.

10 The Scriptures also speak of the calling by God of particular persons, such as David, Elijah, Jeremiah, and Isaiah, so that within the people of God certain special tasks may be performed. They bear witness to the gift of the Spirit or the presence of God enabling them to accomplish God's will and purpose. There

are also profound reflections on what it is to be known and called by God from the very beginning of one's existence (Psalm 139:13–16; Jeremiah 1:4–5). This sense of wonder at the prevenient grace of God is similarly attested in the New Testament, especially in the writings of Paul, when he speaks of those who are "called according to God's purpose", affirming that those whom God "foreknew he also predestined to be conformed to the image of his Son . . . And those whom he predestined he also called; and those whom he called he also justified; and those whom he justified he also glorified" (Romans 8:28–30; cf. 2 Timothy 1:9). The preparation by God for a prophetic task is exemplified in the words spoken by the angel to Zechariah before the birth of John the Baptist: "He will be filled with the Holy Spirit, even from his mother's womb" (Luke 1:15; cf. Judges 13:3–5).

11 Following through the trajectory of the grace of God and the hope for a perfect human response which we have traced in the preceding paragraphs, Christians have, in line with the New Testament writers, seen its culmination in the obedience of Christ. Within this Christological context, they have discerned a similar pattern in the one who would

receive the Word in her heart and in her body, be overshadowed by the Spirit and give birth to the Son of God. The New Testament speaks not only of God's preparation for the birth of the Son, but also of God's election, calling, and sanctification of a Jewish woman in the line of those holy women, such as Sarah and Hannah, whose sons fulfilled the purposes of God for his people. Paul speaks of the Son of God being born "in the fullness of time" and "born of a woman, born under the Law" (Galatians 4:4). The birth of Mary's son is the fulfilment of God's will for Israel, and Mary's part in that fulfilment is that of free and unqualified consent in utter self-giving and trust: "Behold I am the handmaid of the Lord; let it be done to me according to your word" (Luke 1:38; cf. Psalm 123:2).

Mary in Matthew's Birth Narrative

12 While various parts of the New Testament refer to the birth of Christ, only two Gospels, Matthew and Luke, each from its own perspective, narrate the story of his birth and refer specifically to Mary. Matthew entitles his book "the Genesis of Jesus Christ" (1:1) echoing the way the Bible begins (Genesis 1:1). In the genealogy (1:1–18), he traces the genesis of Jesus

back through the Exile to David and ultimately to Abraham. He notes the unlikely role played in the providential ordering of Israel's salvation history by four women, each of whom stretches the boundaries of the Covenant. This emphasis on continuity with the old is counter-balanced in the following account of Jesus' birth by an emphasis on the new (cf. 9:17), a type of re-creation by the Holy Spirit, revealing new possibilities of salvation from sin (1:21) and of the presence of "God with us" (1:23). Matthew stretches the boundaries further in holding together Jesus' Davidic descent through the legal fatherhood of Joseph, and his birth from the Virgin according to Isaiah's prophecy—"Behold a virgin shall conceive and bear a son" (Isaiah 7:14 LXX).

13 In Matthew's account, Mary is mentioned in conjunction with her son in such phrases as "Mary his mother" or "the child and his mother" (2:11, 13, 20, 21). Amid all the political intrigue, murder, and displacement of this tale, one quiet moment of reverence has captured the Christian imagination: the Magi, whose profession it is to know when the time has come, kneel in homage to the infant King with his royal mother (2:2, 11). Matthew emphasizes the continuity of Jesus Christ with Israel's messianic

expectation and the newness that comes with the birth of the Saviour. Descent from David by whatever route, and birth at the ancestral royal city, disclose the first. The virginal conception discloses the second.

Mary in Luke's Birth Narrative

14 In Luke's infancy narrative, Mary is prominent from the beginning. She is the link between John the Baptist and Jesus, whose miraculous births are laid out in deliberate parallel. She receives the angel's message and responds in humble obedience (1:38). She travels on her own from Galilee to Judaea to visit Elizabeth (1:40) and in her song proclaims the eschatological reversal which will be at the heart of her son's proclamation of the Kingdom of God. Mary is the one who in recollection looks beneath the surface of events (2:19, 51) and represents the inwardness of faith and suffering (2:35). She speaks on Joseph's behalf in the scene at the Temple and, although chided for her initial incomprehension, continues to grow in understanding (2:48–51).

15 Within the Lucan narrative, two particular scenes invite reflection on the place of Mary in the life of the Church: the Annunciation and the visit to Elizabeth.

These passages emphasize that Mary is in a unique way the recipient of God's election and grace. The Annunciation story recapitulates several incidents in the Old Testament, notably the births of Isaac (Genesis 18:10–14), Samson (Judges 13:2–5) and Samuel (1 Samuel 1:1–20). The angel's greeting also evokes the passages in Isaiah (66:7–11), Zechariah (9:9), and Zephaniah (3:14–17) that call on the "Daughter of Zion", i.e. Israel awaiting with joy the arrival of her Lord. The choice of "overshadow" (*episkiasei*) to describe the action of the Holy Spirit in the virginal conception (Luke 1:35) echoes the cherubim overshadowing the Ark of the Covenant (Exodus 25:20), the presence of God overshadowing the Tabernacle (Exodus 40:35), and the brooding of the Spirit over the waters at the creation (Genesis 1:2). At the Visitation, Mary's song (*Magnificat*) mirrors the song of Hannah (1 Samuel 2:1–10), broadening its scope so that Mary becomes the one who speaks for all the poor and oppressed who long for God's reign of justice to be established. Just as in Elizabeth's salutation the mother receives a blessing of her own, distinct from that of her child (1:42), so also in the *Magnificat* Mary predicts that "all generations will call me blessed" (1:48). This text provides the scriptural basis for an appropriate devotion to

Mary, though never in separation from her role as mother of the Messiah.

16 In the Annunciation story, the angel calls Mary the Lord's "favoured one" (Greek *kecharitōmenē*, a perfect participle meaning 'one who has been and remains endowed with grace') in a way that implies a prior sanctification by divine grace with a view to her calling. The angel's announcement connects Jesus' being "holy" and "Son of God" with his conception by the Holy Spirit (1:35). The virginal conception then points to the divine sonship of the Saviour who will be born of Mary. The infant not yet born is described by Elizabeth as the Lord: "And why is this granted to me that the mother of my Lord should come to me?" (1:43). The trinitarian pattern of divine action in these scenes is striking: the Incarnation of the Son is initiated by the Father's election of the Blessed Virgin and is mediated by the Holy Spirit. Equally striking is Mary's *fiat*, her 'Amen' given in faith and freedom to God's powerful Word communicated by the angel (1:38).

17 In Luke's account of the birth of Jesus, the praise offered to God by the shepherds parallels the Magi's adoration of the infant in Matthew's account. Again,

this is the scene that constitutes the still centre at the heart of the birth story: "They found Mary and Joseph and the child lying in a manger" (Luke 2:16). In accordance with the Law of Moses, the baby is circumcised and presented in the Temple. On this occasion, Simeon has a special word of prophecy for the mother of the Christ-child, that "a sword will pierce your own soul" (Luke 2:34–35). From this point on Mary's pilgrimage of faith leads to the foot of the cross.

The Virginal Conception

18 The divine initiative in human history is proclaimed in the good news of the virginal conception through the action of the Holy Spirit (Matthew 1:20–3; Luke 1:34–5). The virginal conception may appear in the first place as an absence, i.e. the absence of a human father. It is in reality, however, a sign of the presence and work of the Spirit. Belief in the virginal conception is an early Christian tradition adopted and developed independently by Matthew and Luke.[2] For Christian believers, it is an eloquent sign of the

---

2. Given its strongly Jewish matrix in both Matthean and Lucan versions, an appeal to analogies with pagan mythology or to an exaltation of virginity over the married state to explain the origin of the tradition

divine sonship of Christ and of new life through the Spirit. The virginal conception also points to the new birth of every Christian, as an adopted child of God. Each is "born again (from above) by water and the Spirit" (John 3:3–5). Seen in this light, the virginal conception, far from being an isolated miracle, is a powerful expression of what the Church believes about her Lord, and about our salvation.

Mary and the True Family of Jesus

19 After these birth stories, it comes as something of a surprise to read the episode, narrated in all three Synoptic Gospels, which addresses the question of Jesus' true family. Mark tells us that Jesus' "mother and his brothers" (Mark 3:31) come and stand outside, wanting to speak to him.[3] Jesus in response distances

---

is implausible. Nor is the idea of virginal conception likely to derive from an over-literal reading of the Greek text of Isaiah 7:14 (LXX), for that is not the way the idea is introduced in the Lucan account. Moreover, the suggestion that it originated as an answer to the accusation of illegitimacy levelled at Jesus is unlikely, as that accusation could equally have arisen because it was known that there was something unusual about Jesus' birth (cf. Mark 6:3; John 8:41) and because of the Church's claim about his virginal conception.

3. Although the word 'brother' usually denotes a blood brother, the Greek *adelphos*, like the Hebrew *'ah*, can have a broader meaning of kinsman, or relative (e.g. Genesis 29:12 LXX) or step-brother (e.g. Mark

himself from his natural family: he speaks instead of those gathered around him, his 'eschatological family', that is to say, "whoever does the will of God" (3:35). For Mark, Jesus' natural family, including his own mother, seems at this stage to lack understanding of the true nature of his mission. But that will be the case also with his disciples (e.g. 8:33–5, 9:30–3, 10:35–40). Mark indicates that growth in understanding is inevitably slow and painful, and that genuine faith in Christ is not reached until the encounter with the cross and the empty tomb.

20 In Luke, the stark contrast between the attitude towards Jesus of his natural and eschatological family is avoided (Luke 8:19–21). In a later scene (11:27–8), the woman in the crowd who utters a blessing on his mother, "Blessed is the womb that bore you and the breasts that you sucked", is corrected: "Blessed rather are those who hear the word of God and keep it." But that form of blessing, as Luke sees it, definitely includes Mary who, from the beginning of his

---

6:17f). Relatives who are not siblings could be included in this use of the term at Mark 3:31. Mary did have an extended family: her sister is referred to at John 19:25 and her kinswoman Elizabeth at Luke 1:36. In the early Church different explanations of the references to the 'brothers' of Jesus were given, whether as step-brothers or cousins.

account, was ready to let everything in her life happen according to God's word (1:38).

21 In his second book, the Acts of the Apostles, Luke notes that between the ascension of the Risen Lord and the feast of Pentecost the apostles were gathered in Jerusalem "together with the women and Mary the mother of Jesus, and with his brothers" (Acts 1:14). Mary, who was receptive to the working of God's Spirit at the birth of the Messiah (Luke 1:35–8), is here part of the community of disciples waiting in prayer for the outpouring of the Spirit at the birth of the Church.

Mary in John's Gospel

22 Mary is not mentioned explicitly in the Prologue of John's Gospel. However, something of the significance of her role in salvation history may be discerned by placing her in the context of the considered theological truths that the evangelist articulates in unfolding the good news of the Incarnation. The theological emphasis on the divine initiative, that in the narratives of Matthew and Luke is expressed in the story of Jesus' birth, is paralleled in the Prologue of John by an emphasis on the

predestining will and grace of God by which all those who are brought to new birth are said to be born "not of blood, nor of the will of the flesh, nor of the will of man, but of God" (John 1:13). These are words that could be applied to the birth of Jesus himself.

23 At two important moments of Jesus' public life, the beginning (the wedding at Cana) and the end (the Cross), John notes the presence of Jesus' mother. Each is an hour of need: the first on the surface rather trivial, but at a deeper level a symbolic anticipation of the second. John gives a prominent position in his Gospel to the wedding at Cana (John 2:1–12), calling it the beginning (*archē*) of the signs of Jesus. The account emphasizes the new wine which Jesus brings, symbolising the eschatological marriage feast of God with his people and the messianic banquet of the Kingdom. The story primarily conveys a Christological message: Jesus reveals his messianic glory to his disciples and they believe in him (2:11).

24 The presence of the "mother of Jesus" is mentioned at the beginning of the story: she has a distinctive role in the unfolding of the narrative. Mary seems to

have been invited and be present in her own right, not with "Jesus and his disciples" (John 2:1–2); Jesus is initially seen as present as part of his mother's family. In the dialogue between them when the wine runs out, Jesus seems at first to refuse Mary's implied request, but in the end he accedes to it. This reading of the narrative, however, leaves room for a deeper symbolic reading of the event. In Mary's words "they have no wine", John ascribes to her the expression not so much of a deficiency in the wedding arrangements, as of the longing for salvation of the whole covenant people, who have water for purification but lack the joyful wine of the messianic kingdom. In his answer, Jesus begins by calling into question his former relationship with his mother ("What is there between you and me?"), implying that a change has to take place. He does not address Mary as 'mother', but as "woman" (cf. John 19:26). Jesus no longer sees his relation to Mary as simply one of earthly kinship.

25 Mary's response, to instruct the servants to "Do whatever he tells you" (John 2:5), is unexpected; she is not in charge of the feast (cf. 2:8). Her initial role as the mother of Jesus has radically changed. She herself is now seen as a believer within the messianic community. From this moment on, she commits herself

totally to the Messiah and his word. A new relationship results, indicated by the change in the order of
the main characters at the end of the story: "After
this he went down to Capernaum, with his mother
and his brothers and his disciples" (2:12). The Cana
narrative opens by placing Jesus within the family of
Mary, his mother; from now on, Mary is part of the
"company of Jesus", his disciple. Our reading of this
passage reflects the Church's understanding of the
role of Mary: to help the disciples come to her son,
Jesus Christ, and to "do whatever he tells you."

26 John's second mention of the presence of Mary
occurs at the decisive hour of Jesus' messianic mission,
his crucifixion (19:25–7). Standing with other disciples at the cross, Mary shares in the suffering of
Jesus, who in his last moments addresses a special
word to her, "Woman, behold your son", and to the
beloved disciple, "Behold your mother." We cannot
but be touched that, even in his dying moments,
Jesus is concerned for the welfare of his mother,
showing his filial affection. This surface reading
again invites a symbolic and ecclesial reading of
John's rich narrative. These last commands of Jesus
before he dies reveal an understanding beyond
their primary reference to Mary and "the beloved

disciple" as individuals. The reciprocal roles of the 'woman' and the 'disciple' are related to the identity of the Church. Elsewhere in John, the beloved disciple is presented as the model disciple of Jesus, the one closest to him who never deserted him, the object of Jesus' love, and the ever-faithful witness (13:25, 19:26, 20:1–10, 21:20–5). Understood in terms of discipleship, Jesus' dying words give Mary a motherly role in the Church and encourage the community of disciples to embrace her as a spiritual mother.

27 A corporate understanding of 'woman' also calls the Church constantly to behold Christ crucified, and calls each disciple to care for the Church as mother. Implicit here perhaps is a Mary-Eve typology: just as the first 'woman' was taken from Adam's 'rib' (Genesis 2:22, *pleura* LXX) and became the mother of all the living (Genesis 3:20), so the 'woman' Mary is, on a spiritual level, the mother of all who gain true life from the water and blood that flow from the side (Greek *pleura*, literally 'rib') of Christ (19:34) and from the Spirit that is breathed out from his triumphant sacrifice (19:30, 20:22, cf. 1 John 5:8). In such symbolic and corporate readings, images for the Church, Mary, and discipleship interact with one

another. Mary is seen as the personification of Israel, now giving birth to the Christian community (cf. Isaiah 54:1, 66:7–8), just as she had given birth earlier to the Messiah (cf. Isaiah 7:14). When John's account of Mary at the beginning and end of Jesus' ministry is viewed in this light, it is difficult to speak of the Church without thinking of Mary, the Mother of the Lord, as its archetype and first realisation.

The Woman in Revelation 12

28 In highly symbolic language, full of scriptural imagery, the seer of Revelation describes the vision of a sign in heaven involving a woman, a dragon, and the woman's child. The narrative of Revelation 12 serves to assure the reader of the ultimate victory of God's faithful ones in times of persecution and eschatological struggle. In the course of history, the symbol of the woman has led to a variety of interpretations. Most scholars accept that the primary meaning of the woman is corporate: the people of God, whether Israel, the Church of Christ, or both. Moreover, the narrative style of the author suggests that the 'full picture' of the woman is attained only at the end of the book when the Church of Christ becomes the triumphant New Jerusalem (Revelation 21:1–3). The

actual troubles of the author's community are placed in the frame of history as a whole, which is the scene of the ongoing struggle between the faithful and their enemies, between good and evil, between God and Satan. The imagery of the offspring reminds us of the struggle in Genesis 3:15 between the serpent and the woman, between the serpent's seed and the woman's seed.[4]

29 Given this primary ecclesial interpretation of Revelation 12, is it still possible to find in it a secondary reference to Mary? The text does not explicitly identify the woman with Mary. It refers to the woman as the mother of the "male child who is to rule all the nations with a rod of iron", a citation from

---

4. The Hebrew text of Genesis 3:15 speaks about enmity between the serpent and the woman, and between the offspring of both. The personal pronoun (*hu'*) in the words addressed to the serpent, "He will strike at your head", is masculine. In the Greek translation used by the early Church (LXX), however, the personal pronoun *autos* (he) cannot refer to the offspring (neuter: *to sperma*), but must refer to a masculine individual who could then be the Messiah, born of a woman. The Vulgate (mis)translates the clause as *ipsa conteret caput tuum* ("she will strike at your head"). This feminine pronoun supported a reading of this passage as referring to Mary which has become traditional in the Latin Church. The Neo-Vulgate (1986), however, returns to the neuter *ipsum*, which refers to *semen illius: "Inimicitias ponam inter te et mulierem et semen tuum et semen illius; ipsum conteret caput tuum, et tu conteres calcaneum eius."*

Psalm 2 elsewhere in the New Testament applied to the Messiah as well as to the faithful people of God (cf. Hebrews 1:5, 5:5, Acts 13:33 with Revelation 2:27). In view of this, some Patristic writers came to think of the mother of Jesus when reading this chapter.[5] Given the place of the book of Revelation within the canon of Scripture, in which the different biblical images intertwine, the possibility arose of a more explicit interpretation, both individual and corporate, of Revelation 12, illuminating the place of Mary and the Church in the eschatological victory of the Messiah.

Scriptural Reflection

30 The scriptural witness summons all believers in every generation to call Mary 'blessed'; this Jewish woman of humble status, this daughter of Israel living in hope of justice for the poor, whom God has graced and chosen to become the virgin mother of his Son through the overshadowing of the Holy Spirit. We are to bless her as the 'handmaid of the Lord' who

---

5. Cf. Epiphanius of Salamis (†402), *Panarion* 78.11; Quodvultdeus (†454) *Sermones de Symbolo* III, I.4–6; Oecumenius (†c.550) *Commentarius in Apocalypsin* 6.

gave her unqualified assent to the fulfilment of God's saving plan, as the mother who pondered all things in her heart, as the refugee seeking asylum in a foreign land, as the mother pierced by the innocent suffering of her own child, and as the woman to whom Jesus entrusted his friends. We are at one with her and the apostles, as they pray for the outpouring of the Spirit upon the nascent Church, the eschatological family of Christ. And we may even glimpse in her the final destiny of God's people to share in her son's victory over the powers of evil and death.

B MARY IN THE CHRISTIAN TRADITION

Christ and Mary in the Ancient Common Tradition

31 In the early Church, reflection on Mary served to interpret and safeguard the apostolic Tradition centred on Jesus Christ. Patristic testimony to Mary as 'God-bearer' (*Theotókos*) emerged from reflection on Scripture and the celebration of Christian feasts, but its development was due chiefly to the early Christological controversies. In the crucible of these controversies of the first five centuries, and their resolution in successive Ecumenical Councils, reflection

on Mary's role in the Incarnation was integral to the articulation of orthodox faith in Jesus Christ, true God and true man.

32 In defence of Christ's true humanity, and against Docetism, the early Church emphasized Jesus' birth from Mary. He did not just 'appear' to be human; he did not descend from heaven in a 'heavenly body', nor when he was born did he simply 'pass through' his mother. Rather, Mary gave birth to her son of her own substance. For Ignatius of Antioch (†c.110) and Tertullian (†c.25), Jesus is fully human, because 'truly born' of Mary. In the words of the Nicaeo-Constantinopolitan Creed (381), "he was incarnate of the Holy Spirit and the Virgin Mary, and was made man." The definition of Chalcedon (451), reaffirming this creed, attests that Christ is "consubstantial with the Father according to the divinity and consubstantial with us according to the humanity." The Athanasian Creed confesses yet more concretely that he is "man, of the substance of his Mother." This Anglicans and Roman Catholics together affirm.

33 In defence of his true divinity, the early Church emphasized Mary's virginal conception of Jesus Christ. According to the Fathers, his conception by

the Holy Spirit testifies to Christ's divine origin and divine identity. The One born of Mary is the eternal Son of God. Eastern and Western Fathers—such as Justin (†c.150), Irenaeus (†c.202), Athanasius (†373), and Ambrose (†397)—expounded this New Testament teaching in terms of Genesis 3 (Mary is the antitype of 'virgin Eve') and Isaiah 7:14 (she fulfils the prophet's vision and gives birth to "God with us"). They appealed to the virginal conception to defend both the Lord's divinity and Mary's honour. As the Apostles' Creed confesses: Jesus Christ was "conceived by the Holy Spirit and born of the Virgin Mary." This Anglicans and Roman Catholics together affirm.

34 Mary's title *Theotókos* was formally invoked to safeguard the orthodox doctrine of the unity of Christ's person. This title had been in use in churches under the influence of Alexandria at least from the time of the Arian controversy. Since Jesus Christ is "true God from true God", as the Council of Nicaea (325) declared, these churches concluded that his mother, Mary, can rightly be called the 'God-bearer'. Churches under the influence of Antioch, however, conscious of the threat Apollinarianism posed to belief in the full humanity of Christ, did not immediately adopt this title. The debate between Cyril of

Alexandria (†444) and Nestorius (†455), patriarch of Constantinople, who was formed in the Antiochene school, revealed that the real issue in the question of Mary's title was the unity of Christ's person. The ensuing Council of Ephesus (431) used *Theotókos* (literally 'God-bearer'; in Latin, *Deipara*) to affirm the oneness of Christ's person by identifying Mary as the Mother of God the Word incarnate.[6] The rule of faith on this matter takes more precise expression in the definition of Chalcedon: "One and the same Son . . . was begotten from the Father before the ages as to the divinity and in the latter days for us and our salvation was born as to the humanity from Mary the Virgin *Theotókos*." In receiving the Council of Ephesus and the definition of Chalcedon, Anglicans and Roman Catholics together confess Mary as *Theotókos*.

The Celebration of Mary in the Ancient Common Traditions

35 In the early centuries, communion in Christ included a strong sense of the living presence of the saints as an integral part of the spiritual experience of the

---

6. The Council solemnly approved the content of the Second Letter of Cyril to Nestorius: "It was not that an ordinary man was born first of the holy Virgin, on whom afterwards the Word descended; what we say

churches (Hebrews 12:1, 22–24; Revelation 6:9–11; 7; 8:3–4). Within the 'cloud of witnesses', the Lord's mother came to be seen to have a special place. Themes developed from Scripture and in devotional reflection reveal a deep awareness of Mary's role in the redemption of humanity. Such themes include Mary as Eve's counterpart and as a type of the Church. The response of Christian people, reflecting on these themes, found devotional expression in both private and public prayer.

36 Exegetes delighted in drawing feminine imagery from the Scriptures to contemplate the significance both of the Church and Mary. Fathers as early as Justin Martyr (†c.150) and Irenaeus (†c.202), reflecting on texts like Genesis 3 and Luke 1:26–38, developed, alongside the antithesis of Adam/New Adam, that of Eve/New Eve. Just as Eve is associated with Adam in bringing about our defeat, so Mary is associated with her Son in the conquest of the ancient enemy (cf. Genesis 3:15, *vide supra* footnote 4): 'virgin' Eve's disobedience results in death; the virgin

---

is that: being united with the flesh from the womb, the Word has undergone birth in the flesh . . . therefore the Holy Fathers had the courage to call the Holy Virgin *Theotókos*"(DS 251).

Mary's obedience opens the way to salvation. The New Eve shares in the New Adam's victory over sin and death.

37 The Fathers presented Mary the Virgin Mother as a model of holiness for consecrated virgins, and increasingly taught that she had remained 'Ever-Virgin'.[7] In their reflection, virginity was understood not only as physical integrity, but as an interior disposition of openness, obedience, and single-hearted fidelity to Christ which models Christian discipleship and issues in spiritual fruitfulness.

38 In this patristic understanding, Mary's virginity was closely related to her sanctity. Although some early

---

7. The Tome of Leo, which was decisive for the outcome of the Council of Chalcedon (451), states that Christ "was conceived by the Holy Spirit in the womb of the Virgin Mother, who gave him birth without losing her virginity, as she conceived him without losing her virginity" (DS 291). Similarly Athanasius speaks in *De Virginitate* (*Le Muséon* 42: 244.248) of "Mary, who . . . remained a virgin to the end [as a model for] all to come after her." Cf. John Chrysostom (†407) *Homily on Matthew* 5,3. The first Ecumenical Council to use the term *Aeiparthenos* (*semper virgo*) was the Second Council of Constantinople (553). This designation is already implicit in the classical Western formulation of Mary's *virginitas as ante partum, in partu, post partum*. This tradition appears consistently in the Western Church from Ambrose onward. As Augustine wrote, "she conceived him as a virgin, she gave birth as a virgin, she remained a virgin" (*Sermo* 51.18; cf. *Sermo* 196.1).

exegetes thought that Mary was not wholly without sin,[8] Augustine (†430) witnessed to contemporary reluctance to speak of any sin in her.

> We must except the holy Virgin Mary, concerning whom I wish to raise no question when it touches the subject of sins, out of honour to the Lord; for from him we know what abundance of grace for overcoming sin in every particular was conferred on her who had the merit to conceive and bear him who undoubtedly had no sin. (*De natura et gratia* 36.42)

Other Fathers from West and East, appealing to the angelic salutation (Luke 1:28) and Mary's response (Luke 1:38), support the view that Mary was filled with grace from her origin in anticipation of her unique vocation as Mother of the Lord. By the fifth century they hail her as a new creation: blameless, spotless, "holy in body and soul" (Theodotus of Ancyra, *Homily* 6, 11: †before 446). By the sixth

---

8. Thus Irenaeus criticizes her for "excessive haste" at Cana, "seeking to push her son into performing a miracle before his hour had come" (*Adv. Haer.* III.16.7); Origen speaks of her wavering in faith at the cross, "so she too would have some sin for which Christ died" (*Hom. in Lc*, 17,6). Suggestions like these are found in the writings of Tertullian, Ambrose, and John Chrysostom.

century, the title *panaghia* ('all-holy') can be found in the East.

39 Following the Christological debates at the councils of Ephesus and Chalcedon, devotion to Mary flourished. When the patriarch of Antioch refused Mary the title of *Theotókos*, Emperor Leo I (457–74) commanded the patriarch of Constantinople to insert this title into the eucharistic prayer throughout the East. By the sixth century, commemoration of Mary as 'God-bearer' had become universal in the eucharistic prayers of East and West (with the exception of the Assyrian Church of the East). Texts and images celebrating Mary's holiness were multiplied in liturgical poetry and songs, such as the *Akathist*, a hymn probably written soon after Chalcedon and still sung in the Eastern church. A tradition of praying with and praising Mary was thus gradually established. This has been associated since the fourth century, especially in the East, with asking for her protection.[9]

---

9. Witness the invocation of Mary in the early text known traditionally as *Sub tuum praesidium*: Ὑπὸ τὴν σὴν εὐσπλαγνίαν καταφεύγομεν, Θεοτόκε τὰς ἡμῶν ἱκεσίας μὴ παρίδῃς ἐν περιστάσει, ἀλλ' ἐκ κινδύνου ῥῦσαι ἡμᾶς, μόνη ἁγνή, μόνη εὐλογημένη. (Cf. O. Stegemüller, *Sub tuum praesidium. Bemerkungen zur ältesten Überlieferung*, in: *ZKTh* 74 [1952], pp. 76–82 [77]). This text (with two changes) is used to this day in the

40 After the Council of Ephesus, churches began to be dedicated to Mary and feasts in her honour began to be celebrated on particular days in these churches. Prompted by popular piety and gradually adopted by local churches, feasts celebrating Mary's conception (8/9 December), birth (8 September), presentation (21 November), and dormition (15 August) mirrored the liturgical commemorations of events in the life of the Lord. They drew both on the canonical Scriptures and also on apocryphal accounts of Mary's early life and her 'falling asleep'. A feast of the conception of Mary can be dated in the East to the late seventh century, and was introduced into the Western church through southern England in the early eleventh century. It drew on popular devotion expressed in the second-century *Protoevangelium of James*, and paralleled the dominical feast of the Annunciation and the existing feast of the conception of John the Baptist. The feast of Mary's 'falling asleep' dates from the end of the sixth century, but

---

Greek liturgical tradition; versions of this prayer also occur in the Ambrosian, Roman, Byzantine, and Coptic liturgies. A familiar English version is: "We fly to thy protection, O holy Mother of God; despise not our petitions in our necessities but deliver us from all dangers, O ever glorious and blessed Virgin."

was influenced by legendary narratives of the end of
Mary's life already widely in circulation. In the West,
the most influential of them are the *Transitus Mariae*.
In the East, the feast was known as the 'dormition',
which implied her death but did not exclude her
being taken into heaven. In the West, the term used
was 'assumption', which emphasized her being taken
into heaven but did not exclude the possibility of her
dying. Belief in her assumption was grounded in the
promise of the resurrection of the dead and the
recognition of Mary's dignity as *Theotókos* and 'Ever
Virgin', coupled with the conviction that she who
had borne Life should be associated to her Son's victory over death, and with the glorification of his
Body, the Church.

The Growth of Marian Doctrine and Devotion in the Middle Ages

41 The spread of these feasts of Mary gave rise to homilies in which preachers delved into the Scriptures,
searching for types and motifs to illuminate the
Virgin's place in the economy of salvation. During
the High Middle Ages a growing emphasis on the
humanity of Christ was matched by attention to the
exemplary virtues of Mary. Bernard, for example,

articulates this emphasis in his homilies. Meditation on the lives of both Christ and Mary became increasingly popular, and gave rise to the development of such devotional practices as the rosary. The paintings, sculptures, and stained glass of the High and Late Middle Ages lent to this devotion immediacy and colour.

42 During these centuries there were some major shifts of emphasis in theological reflection about Mary. Theologians of the High Middle Ages developed patristic reflection on Mary as a 'type' of the Church, and also as the New Eve, in a way that associated her ever more closely with Christ in the continuing work of redemption. The centre of attention of believers shifted from Mary as representing the faithful Church, and so also redeemed humanity, to Mary as dispensing Christ's graces to the faithful. Scholastic theologians in the West developed an increasingly elaborate body of doctrine about Mary in her own right. Much of this doctrine grew out of speculation about the holiness and sanctification of Mary. Questions about this were influenced not only by the scholastic theology of grace and original sin, but also by presuppositions concerning procreation and the relation between soul and body. For example, if she

were sanctified in the womb of her mother, more perfectly even than John the Baptist and Jeremiah, some theologians thought that the precise moment of her sanctification had to be determined according to the current understanding of when the 'rational soul' was infused into the body. Theological developments in the Western doctrine of grace and sin raised other questions: how could Mary be free of all sin, including original sin, without jeopardising the role of Christ as universal Saviour? Speculative reflection led to intense discussions about how Christ's redeeming grace may have preserved Mary from original sin. The measured theology of Mary's sanctification found in the *Summa Theologiae* of Thomas Aquinas, and the subtle reasoning of Duns Scotus about Mary, were deployed in extended controversy over whether Mary was immaculate from the first moment of her conception.

43 In the Late Middle Ages, scholastic theology grew increasingly apart from spirituality. Less and less rooted in scriptural exegesis, theologians relied on logical probability to establish their positions, and Nominalists speculated on what could be done by the absolute power and will of God. Spirituality, no longer in creative tension with theology, emphasized

affectivity and personal experience. In popular religion, Mary came widely to be viewed as an intermediary between God and humanity, and even as a worker of miracles with powers that verged on the divine. This popular piety in due course influenced the theological opinions of those who had grown up with it, and who subsequently elaborated a theological rationale for the florid Marian devotion of the Late Middle Ages.

From the Reformation to the Present Day

44 One powerful impulse for Reformation in the early sixteenth century was a widespread reaction against devotional practices which approached Mary as a mediatrix alongside Christ, or sometimes even in his place. Such exaggerated devotions, in part inspired by presentations of Christ as inaccessible Judge as well as Redeemer, were sharply criticized by Erasmus and Thomas More and decisively rejected by the Reformers. Together with a radical re-reception of Scripture as the fundamental touchstone of divine revelation, there was a re-reception by the Reformers of the belief that Jesus Christ is the only mediator between God and humanity. This entailed a rejection of real and perceived abuses surrounding devotion to

Mary. It led also to the loss of some positive aspects of devotion and the diminution of her place in the life of the Church.

45 In this context, the English Reformers continued to receive the doctrine of the ancient church concerning Mary. Their positive teaching about Mary concentrated on her role in the Incarnation: it is summed up in their acceptance of her as the *Theotókos*, because this was seen to be both scriptural and in accord with ancient common tradition. Following the traditions of the early Church and other Reformers like Martin Luther, the English Reformers such as Latimer (*Works*, 2:105), Cranmer (*Works*, 2:60; 2:88), and Jewel (*Works*, 3:440–1) accepted that Mary was 'Ever Virgin'. Following Augustine, they showed a reticence about affirming that Mary was a sinner. Their chief concern was to emphasize the unique sinlessness of Christ, and the need of all humankind, including Mary, for a Saviour (cf. Luke 1:47). Articles IX and XV affirmed the universality of human sinfulness. They neither affirmed nor denied the possibility of Mary having been preserved by grace from participation in this general human condition. It is notable that the *Book of Common Prayer* in the Christmas collect and preface refers to Mary as 'a pure virgin'.

46 From 1561, the calendar of the Church of England (which was reproduced in the 1662 *Book of Common Prayer*) contained five feasts associated with Mary: Conception of Mary, Nativity of Mary, Annunciation, Visitation, and Purification/Presentation. There was, however, no longer a feast of the Assumption (15 August): not only was it understood to lack scriptural warrant, but was also seen as exalting Mary at the expense of Christ. Anglican liturgy, as expressed in the successive *Books of Common Prayer* (1549, 1552, 1559, 1662) when it mentions Mary, gives prominence to her role as the 'pure Virgin' from whose 'substance' the Son took human nature (cf. Article II). In spite of the diminution of devotion to Mary in the sixteenth century, reverence for her endured in the continued use of the *Magnificat* in Evening Prayer, and the unchanged dedication of ancient churches and Lady Chapels. In the seventeenth century writers such as Lancelot Andrewes, Jeremy Taylor, and Thomas Ken re-appropriated from patristic tradition a fuller appreciation of the place of Mary in the prayers of the believer and of the Church. For example, Andrewes in his *Preces Privatae* borrowed from Eastern liturgies when he showed a warmth of Marian devotion "Commemorating the all holy, immaculate, more than blessed mother of God and evervirgin Mary."

This re-appropriation can be traced into the next century, and into the Oxford Movement of the nineteenth century.

47 In the Roman Catholic Church, the continued growth of Marian doctrine and devotion, while moderated by the reforming decrees of the Council of Trent (1545–63), also suffered the distorting influence of Protestant-Catholic polemics. To be Roman Catholic came to be identified by an emphasis on devotion to Mary. The depth and popularity of Marian spirituality in the nineteenth and the first half of the twentieth centuries contributed to the definitions of the dogmas of the Immaculate Conception (1854) and the Assumption (1950). On the other hand, the pervasiveness of this spirituality began to give rise to criticism both within and beyond the Roman Catholic Church and initiated a process of re-reception. This re-reception was evident in the Second Vatican Council which, consonant with the contemporary biblical, patristic, and liturgical renewals, and with concern for ecumenical sensitivities, chose not to draft a separate document on Mary, but to integrate doctrine about her into the Constitution on the Church, *Lumen Gentium* (1964)—more specifically, into its final section

describing the eschatological pilgrimage of the Church (Chapter VIII). The Council intended "to explain carefully both the role of the Blessed Virgin in the mystery of the Word Incarnate and of the Mystical Body, as well as the duties of the redeemed human race towards the God-bearer, mother of Christ and mother of humanity, especially of the faithful" (art. 54). *Lumen Gentium* concludes by calling Mary a sign of hope and comfort for God's pilgrim people (art. 68–9). The Fathers of the Council consciously sought to resist exaggerations by returning to patristic emphases and placing Marian doctrine and devotion in its proper Christological and ecclesial context.

48 Soon after the Council, faced by an unanticipated decline in devotion to Mary, Pope Paul VI published an Apostolic Exhortation, *Marialis Cultus* (1974), to remove doubts about the Council's intentions and to foster appropriate Marian devotion. His review of the place of Mary in the revised Roman rite showed that she has not been 'demoted' by the liturgical renewal, but that devotion to her is properly located within the Christological focus of the Church's public prayer. He reflected on Mary as "a model of the spiritual attitudes with which the Church celebrates

and lives the divine mysteries" (art. 16). She is the model for the whole Church, but also a "teacher of the spiritual life for individual Christians" (art. 21). According to Paul VI, the authentic renewal of Marian devotion must be integrated with the doctrines of God, Christ, and the Church. Devotion to Mary must be in accordance with the Scriptures and the liturgy of the Church; it must be sensitive to the concerns of other Christians and it must affirm the full dignity of women in public and private life. The Pope also issued cautions to those who err either by exaggeration or neglect. Finally, he commended the recitation of the *Angelus* and the Rosary as traditional devotions which are compatible with these norms. In 2002, Pope John Paul II reinforced the Christological focus of the Rosary by proposing five 'mysteries of Light' from the Gospels' account of Christ's public ministry between his Baptism and Passion. "The Rosary", he states, "though clearly Marian in character, is at heart a Christocentric prayer" (*Rosarium Virginis Mariae*, 1).

49 Mary has a new prominence in Anglican worship through the liturgical renewals of the twentieth century. In most Anglican prayer books, Mary is again mentioned by name in the Eucharistic prayers.

Plate 1: Dormition of the Virgin; Russian – Novgorod School, fifteenth century (courtesy of Temple Gallery, London). The icon depicts the Risen Lord holding Mary's soul at the moment of her death. Icons, which play an important role in the worship of the Eastern Churches, are increasingly familiar to Catholics and Anglicans.

Plate 2: Anglican: St Luke's, Sydney, Australia (Aboriginal)

Plate 3: Anglican: Monmouth, Wales (Celtic)

Plate 4: Anglican: Newcastle Upon Tyne, England
St Nicholas Cathedral, Mothers' Union Banner

Plate 5: Anglican: Gibraltar Cathedral – Wall image

Plate 6: Roman Catholic: Malta (Artist, Michael Evsk)

Plate 7: Roman Catholic: Via Dolorosa;
The Fourth Station of the Cross, Old City, Jerusalem.

Plate 8: Roman Catholic: Nativity window in the Church of
St Catherine, Manger Square, Bethlehem, Palestine.

Further, 15 August has come to be widely celebrated as a principal feast in honour of Mary with Scripture readings, collect, and proper preface. Other feasts associated with Mary have also been renewed, and liturgical resources offered for use on these festivals. Given the definitive role of authorized liturgical texts and practices in Anglican formularies, such developments are highly significant.

50 The above developments show that in recent decades a re-reception of the place of Mary in corporate worship has been taking place across the Anglican Communion. At the same time, in *Lumen Gentium* (Chapter VIII) and the Exhortation *Marialis Cultus* the Roman Catholic Church has attempted to set devotion to Mary within the context of the teaching of Scripture and the ancient common tradition. This constitutes, for the Roman Catholic Church, a re-reception of teaching about Mary. Revision of the calendars and lectionaries used in our Communions, especially the liturgical provision associated with feasts of Mary, gives evidence of a shared process of re-receiving the scriptural testimony to her place in the faith and life of the Church. Growing ecumenical exchange has contributed to the process of re-reception in both Communions.

51 The Scriptures lead us together to praise and bless Mary as the handmaid of the Lord, who was providentially prepared by divine grace to be the mother of our Redeemer. Her unqualified assent to the fulfilment of God's saving plan can be seen the supreme instance of a believer's 'Amen' in response to the 'Yes' of God. She stands as a model of holiness, obedience, and faith for all Christians. As one who received the Word in her heart and in her body, and brought it forth into the world, Mary belongs in the prophetic tradition. We are agreed in our belief in the Blessed Virgin Mary as *Theotókos*. Our two communions are both heirs to a rich tradition which recognizes Mary as ever virgin, and sees her as the new Eve and as a type of the Church. We join in praying and praising with Mary whom all generations have called blessed, in observing her festivals and according her honour in the communion of the saints, and are agreed that Mary and the saints pray for the whole Church (see below in section D). In all of this, we see Mary as inseparably linked with Christ and the Church. Within this broad consideration of the role of Mary, we now focus on the theology of hope and grace.

C MARY WITHIN THE PATTERN OF GRACE AND HOPE

52 Participation in the glory of God, through the mediation of the Son, in the power of the Spirit is the Gospel hope (cf. 2 Corinthians 3:18; 4:4–6). The Church already enjoys this hope and destiny through the Holy Spirit, who is the 'pledge' of our inheritance in Christ (Ephesians 1:14, 2 Corinthians 5:5). For Paul especially, what it means to be fully human can only be understood rightly when it is viewed in the light of what we are to become in Christ, the 'last Adam', as opposed to what we had become in the old Adam (1 Corinthians 15:42–9, cf. Romans 5:12–21). This eschatological perspective sees Christian life in terms of the vision of the exalted Christ leading believers to cast off sins that entangle (Hebrews 12:1–2) and to participate in his purity and love, made available through his atoning sacrifice (1 John 3:3, 4:10). We thus view the economy of grace from its fulfilment in Christ 'back' into history, rather than 'forward' from its beginning in fallen creation towards the future in Christ. This perspective offers fresh light in which to consider the place of Mary.

53 The hope of the Church is based upon the testimony it has received about the present glory of Christ. The Church proclaims that Christ was not only raised bodily from the tomb, but was exalted to the right hand of the Father, to share in the Father's glory (1 Timothy 3:16, 1 Peter 1:21). Insofar as believers are united with Christ in baptism and share in Christ's sufferings (Romans 6:1–6), they participate through the Spirit in his glory, and are raised up with him in anticipation of the final revelation (cf. Romans 8:17, Ephesians 2:6, Colossians 3:1). It is the destiny of the Church and of its members, the "saints" chosen in Christ "before the foundation of the world", to be "holy and blameless" and to share in the glory of Christ (Ephesians 1:3–5, 5:27). Paul speaks as it were from the future retrospectively, when he says, "those whom God predestined he also called; and those whom he called he also justified; and those whom he justified he also glorified" (Romans 8:30). In the succeeding chapters of Romans, Paul explicates this many-faceted drama of God's election in Christ, keeping in view its end: the inclusion of the Gentiles, so that "all Israel will be saved" (Romans 11:26).

Mary in the Economy of Grace

54 Within this biblical framework we have considered afresh the distinctive place of the Virgin Mary in the economy of grace, as the one who bore Christ, the elect of God. The word of God delivered by Gabriel addresses her as already 'graced', inviting her to respond in faith and freedom to God's call (Luke 1:28, 38, 45). The Spirit is operative within her in the conception of the Saviour, and this "blessed among women" is inspired to sing "all generations will call me blessed" (Luke 1:42, 48). Viewed eschatologically, Mary thus embodies the 'elect Israel' of whom Paul speaks—glorified, justified, called, predestined. This is the pattern of grace and hope which we see at work in the life of Mary, who holds a distinctive place in the common destiny of the Church as the one who bore in her own flesh 'the Lord of glory'. Mary is marked out from the beginning as the one chosen, called, and graced by God through the Holy Spirit for the task that lay ahead of her.

55 The Scriptures tell us of barren women who were gifted by God with children—Rachel, Manoah's

wife, Hannah (Genesis 30:1–24, Judges 13, 1 Samuel 1), and those past childbearing—Sarah (Genesis 18:9–15, 21:1–7), and most notably Mary's cousin, Elizabeth (Luke 1:7, 24). These women highlight the singular role of Mary, who was neither barren nor past child-bearing age, but a fruitful virgin: in her womb the Spirit brought about the conception of Jesus. The Scriptures also speak of God's care for all human beings, even before their coming to birth (Psalm 139:13–18), and recount the action of God's grace preceding the specific calling of particular persons, even from their conception (cf. Jeremiah 4:5, Luke 1:15, Galatians 1:15). With the early Church, we see in Mary's acceptance of the divine will the fruit of her prior preparation, signified in Gabriel's affirmation of her as 'graced'. We can thus see that God was at work in Mary from her earliest beginnings, preparing her for the unique vocation of bearing in her own flesh the new Adam, in whom all things in heaven and earth hold together (cf. Colossians 1:16–17). Of Mary, both personally and as a representative figure, we can say she is "God's workmanship, created in Christ Jesus for good works which God prepared beforehand" (Ephesians 2:10).

56 Mary, a pure virgin, bore God incarnate in her womb. Her bodily intimacy with her son was all of a piece with her faithful following of him, and her maternal participation in his victorious self-giving (Luke 2:35). All this is clearly testified in Scripture, as we have seen. There is no direct testimony in Scripture concerning the end of Mary's life. However, certain passages give instances of those who follow God's purposes faithfully being drawn into God's presence. Moreover, these passages offer hints or partial analogies that may throw light on the mystery of Mary's entry into glory. For instance, the biblical pattern of anticipated eschatology appears in the account of Stephen, the first martyr (Acts 7:54–60). At the moment of his death, which conforms to that of his Lord, he sees "the glory of God, and Jesus" the "Son of Man" not seated in judgement, but "standing at the right hand of God" to welcome his faithful servant. Similarly, the penitent thief who calls on the crucified Christ is accorded the special promise of being with Christ immediately in Paradise (Luke 23:43). God's faithful servant Elijah is taken up by a whirlwind into heaven (2 Kings 2:11), and of Enoch it is written, "he was attested as having pleased God" as a man of faith, and

was therefore "taken up so that he should not see death; and he was not found because God had taken him" (Hebrews 11:5, cf. Genesis 5:24). Within such a pattern of anticipated eschatology, Mary can also be seen as the faithful disciple fully present with God in Christ. In this way, she is a sign of hope for all humanity.

57 The pattern of hope and grace already foreshadowed in Mary will be fulfilled in the new creation in Christ when all the redeemed will participate in the full glory of the Lord (cf. 2 Corinthians 3:18). Christian experience of communion with God in this present life is a sign and foretaste of divine grace and glory, a hope shared with the whole of creation (Romans 8:18–23). The individual believer and the Church find their consummation in the new Jerusalem, the holy bride of Christ (cf. Revelation 21:2, Ephesians 5:27). When Christians from East and West through the generations have pondered God's work in Mary, they have discerned in faith (cf. *Gift*, 29) that it is fitting that the Lord gathered her wholly to himself: in Christ, she is already a new creation in whom "the old has passed away and the new has come" (2 Corinthians 5:17). Viewed from such an eschatological perspective, Mary may be seen

both as a type of the Church, and as a disciple with a special place in the economy of salvation.

The Papal Definitions

58 Thus far we have outlined our common faith concerning the place of Mary in the divine purpose. Roman Catholic Christians, however, are bound to believe the teaching defined by Pope Pius XII in 1950: "that the Immaculate Mother of God, the ever-Virgin Mary, having completed the course of her earthly life, was assumed body and soul into heavenly glory." We note that the dogma does not adopt a particular position as to how Mary's life ended,[10] nor does it use about her the language of death and resurrection, but celebrates the action of

---

10. The reference in the dogma to Mary being assumed 'body and soul' has caused difficulty for some, on historical and philosophical grounds. The dogma leaves open, however, the question as to what the absence of her mortal remains means in historical terms. Likewise, 'assumed body and soul' is not intended to privilege a particular anthropology. More positively, 'assumed body and soul' can be seen to have Christological and ecclesiological implications. Mary as 'God-bearer' is intimately, indeed bodily, related to Christ: his own bodily glorification now embraces hers. And, since Mary bore his body of flesh, she is intimately related to the Church, Christ's body. In brief, the formulation of the dogma responds to theological rather than historical or philosophical questions in relation to Mary.

God in her. Thus, given the understanding we have reached concerning the place of Mary in the economy of hope and grace, we can affirm together the teaching that God has taken the Blessed Virgin Mary in the fullness of her person into his glory as consonant with Scripture and that it can, indeed, only be understood in the light of Scripture. Roman Catholics can recognize that this teaching about Mary is contained in the dogma. While the calling and destiny of all the redeemed is their glorification in Christ, Mary, as *Theotókos*, holds the pre-eminent place within the communion of saints and embodies the destiny of the Church.

59 Roman Catholics are also bound to believe that "the most blessed Virgin Mary was, from the first moment of her conception, by a singular grace and privilege of almighty God and in view of the merits of Christ Jesus the Saviour of the human race, preserved immune from all stain of original sin" (Dogma of the Immaculate Conception of Mary, defined by Pope Pius IX, 1854).[11] The definition teaches that Mary,

---

11. The definition addressed an old controversy about the timing of the sanctification of Mary, in affirming that this took place at the very first moment of her conception.

like all other human beings, has need of Christ as her Saviour and Redeemer (cf. *Lumen Gentium* 53; *Catechism of the Catholic Church* 491). The negative notion of 'sinlessness' runs the risk of obscuring the fullness of Christ's saving work. It is not so much that Mary lacks something which other human beings 'have', namely sin, but that the glorious grace of God filled her life from the beginning.[12] The holiness which is our end in Christ (cf. 1 John 3:2–3) was seen, by unmerited grace, in Mary, who is the proto-type of the hope of grace for humankind as a whole. According to the New Testament, being 'graced' has the connotation of being freed from sin through Christ's blood (Ephesians 1:6–7). The Scriptures point to the efficacy of Christ's atoning sacrifice even for those who preceded him in time (cf. 1 Peter 3:19, John 8:56, 1 Corinthians 10:4). Here again the escha-tological perspective illuminates our understanding of Mary's person and calling. In view of her vocation to

---

12. The assertion of Paul at Romans 3:23—"all have sinned and fall short of the glory of God"—might appear to allow for no exceptions, not even for Mary. However, it is important to note the rhetorical-apologetic context of the general argument of Romans 1–3, which is concerned to show the equal sinfulness of Jews and Gentiles (3:9). Romans 3:23 has a quite specific purpose in context which is unrelated to the issue of the 'sinlessness' or otherwise of Mary.

be the mother of the Holy One (Luke 1:35), we can affirm together that Christ's redeeming work reached 'back' in Mary to the depths of her being, and to her earliest beginnings. This is not contrary to the teaching of Scripture, and can only be understood in the light of Scripture. Roman Catholics can recognize in this what is affirmed by the dogma—namely "preserved from all stain of original sin" and "from the first moment of her conception."

60 We have agreed together that the teaching about Mary in the two definitions of 1854 and 1950, understood within the biblical pattern of the economy of grace and hope outlined here, can be said to be consonant with the teaching of the Scriptures and the ancient common traditions. However, in Roman Catholic understanding as expressed in these two definitions, the proclamation of any teaching as dogma implies that the teaching in question is affirmed to be "revealed by God" and therefore to be believed "firmly and constantly" by all the faithful (i.e. it is *de fide*). The problem which the dogmas may present for Anglicans can be put in terms of Article VI:

> Holy Scripture containeth all things necessary to salvation: so that whatsoever is not read

> therein, nor may be proved thereby, is not to be
> required of any man, that it should be believed
> as an article of the Faith, or be thought requi-
> site or necessary to salvation.

We agree that nothing can be required to be believed as an article of faith unless it is revealed by God. The question arises for Anglicans, however, as to whether these doctrines concerning Mary are revealed by God in a way which must be held by believers as a matter of faith.

61 The particular circumstances and precise formulations of the 1854 and 1950 definitions have created
problems not only for Anglicans but also for other
Christians. The formulations of these doctrines and
some objections to them are situated within the
thought-forms of their time. In particular, the phrases
"revealed by God" (1854) and "divinely revealed"
(1950) used in the dogmas reflect the theology of
revelation that was dominant in the Roman Catholic
Church at the time that the definitions were made,
and which found authoritative expression in the
Constitution *Dei Filius* of the First Vatican Council.
They have to be understood today in the light of the
way this teaching was refined by the Second Vatican

Council in its Constitution *Dei Verbum*, particularly in regard to the central role of Scripture in the reception and transmission of revelation. When the Roman Catholic Church affirms that a truth is "revealed by God", there is no suggestion of new revelation. Rather, the definitions are understood to bear witness to what has been revealed from the beginning. The Scriptures bear normative witness to such revelation (cf. *Gift* 19). This revelation is received by the community of believers and transmitted in time and place through the Scriptures and through the preaching, liturgy, spirituality, life, and teaching of the Church, that draw upon the Scriptures. In *The Gift of Authority* the Commission sought to explicate a method by which such authoritative teaching could arise, the key point being that it needs to be in conformity with Scripture, which remains a primary concern for Anglicans and Roman Catholics alike.

62 Anglicans have also questioned whether these doctrines must be held by believers as a matter of faith in view of the fact that the Bishop of Rome defined these doctrines "independent of a Council" (cf. *Authority II*. 30). In response, Roman Catholics have pointed to the *sensus fidelium*, the liturgical tradition throughout the local churches, and the active support

of the Roman Catholic bishops (cf. *Gift* 29–30): these were the elements through which these doctrines were recognized as belonging to the faith of the Church, and therefore able to be defined (cf. *Gift* 47). For Roman Catholics, it belongs to the office of the Bishop of Rome that he should be able, under strictly limited conditions, to make such a definition (cf. *Pastor Aeternus* (1870); DS 3069–70). The definitions of 1854 and 1950 were not made in response to controversy, but gave voice to the consensus of faith among believers in communion with the Bishop of Rome. They were re-affirmed by the Second Vatican Council. For Anglicans, it would be the consent of an ecumenical council which, teaching according to the Scriptures, most securely demonstrates that the necessary conditions for a teaching to be *de fide* had been met. Where this is the case, as with the definition of the *Theotókos*, both Roman Catholics and Anglicans would agree that the witness of the Church is firmly and constantly to be believed by all the faithful (cf. 1 John 1:1–3).

63 Anglicans have asked whether it would be a condition of the future restoration of full communion that they should be required to accept the definitions of 1854 and 1950. Roman Catholics find it hard to

envisage a restoration of communion in which acceptance of certain doctrines would be requisite for some and not for others. In addressing these issues, we have been mindful that "one consequence of our separation has been a tendency for Anglicans and Roman Catholics alike to exaggerate the importance of the Marian dogmas in themselves at the expense of the other truths more closely related to the foundation of the Christian faith" (*Authority II*, 30). Anglicans and Roman Catholics agree that the doctrines of the Assumption and the Immaculate Conception of Mary must be understood in the light of the more central truth of her identity as *Theotókos*, which itself depends on faith in the Incarnation. We recognize that, following the Second Vatican Council and the teaching of recent Popes, the Christological and ecclesiological context for the Church's doctrine concerning Mary is being re-received within the Roman Catholic Church. We now suggest that the adoption of an eschatological perspective may deepen our shared understanding of the place of Mary in the economy of grace, and the tradition of the Church concerning Mary which both our communions receive. Our hope is that the Roman Catholic Church and the Anglican Communion will recognize a common faith in the agreement concerning

Mary which we here offer. Such a re-reception would mean the Marian teaching and devotion within our respective communities, including differences of emphasis, would be seen to be authentic expressions of Christian belief.[13] Any such re-reception would have to take place within the context of a mutual re-reception of an effective teaching authority in the Church, such as that set out in *The Gift of Authority*.

D Mary in the life of the Church

64 "All the promises of God find their 'Yes' in Christ: that is why we offer the 'Amen' through him, to the glory of God" (2 Corinthians 1:20). God's 'Yes' in Christ takes a distinctive and demanding form as it is

---

13. In such circumstances, the explicit acceptance of the precise wording of the definitions of 1854 and 1950 might not be required of believers who were not in communion with Rome when they were defined. Conversely, Anglicans would have to accept that the definitions are a legitimate expression of Catholic faith, and are to be respected as such, even if these formulations were not employed by them. There are instances in ecumenical agreement in which what one partner has defined as *de fide* can be expressed by another partner in a different way, as for example in the *Common Christological Declaration between the Catholic Church and the Assyrian Church of the East* (1994) or the *Joint Declaration on the Doctrine of Justification between the Roman Catholic Church and the Lutheran World Federation* (1999).

addressed to Mary. The profound mystery of "Christ in you, the hope of glory" (Colossians 1:27) has a unique meaning for her. It enables her to speak the 'Amen' in which, through the Spirit's overshadowing, God's 'Yes' of new creation is inaugurated. As we have seen, this *fiat* of Mary was distinctive, in its openness to God's Word, and in the path to the foot of the cross and beyond on which the Spirit led her. The Scriptures portray Mary as growing in her relationship with Christ: his sharing of her natural family (Luke 2:39) was transcended in her sharing of his eschatological family, those upon whom the Spirit is poured out (Acts 1:14, 2:1–4). Mary's 'Amen' to God's 'Yes' in Christ to her is thus both unique and a model for every disciple and for the life of the Church.

65 One outcome of our study has been awareness of differences in the ways in which the example of Mary living out the grace of God has been appropriated into the devotional lives of our traditions. Whilst both traditions have recognized her special place in the communion of saints, different emphases have marked the way we have experienced her ministry. Anglicans have tended to begin from reflection on the scriptural example of Mary as an inspiration and model for discipleship. Roman Catholics have

given prominence to the ongoing ministry of Mary in the economy of grace and the communion of saints. Mary points people to Christ, commending them to him and helping them to share his life. Neither of these general characterizations do full justice to the richness and diversity of either tradition, and the twentieth century witnessed a particular growth in convergence as many Anglicans were drawn into a more active devotion to Mary, and Roman Catholics discovered afresh the scriptural roots of such devotion. We together agree that in understanding Mary as the fullest human example of the life of grace, we are called to reflect on the lessons of her life recorded in Scripture and to join with her as one indeed not dead, but truly alive in Christ. In doing so we walk together as pilgrims in communion with Mary, Christ's foremost disciple, and all those whose participation in the new creation encourages us to be faithful to our calling (cf. 2 Corinthians 5:17, 19).

66 Aware of the distinctive place of Mary in the history of salvation, Christians have given her a special place in their liturgical and private prayer, praising God for what he has done in and through her. In singing the *Magnificat*, they praise God with her; in

the Eucharist, they pray with her as they do with all God's people, integrating their prayers in the great communion of saints. They recognize Mary's place in "the prayer of all the saints" that is being uttered before the throne of God in the heavenly liturgy (Revelation 8:3–4). All these ways of including Mary in praise and prayer belong to our common heritage, as does our acknowledgement of her unique status as *Theotókos*, which gives her a distinctive place within the communion of saints.

Intercession and Mediation in the Communion of Saints

67 The practice of believers asking Mary to intercede for them with her son grew rapidly following her being declared *Theotókos* at the Council of Ephesus. The most common form today of such intercession is the 'Hail Mary'. This form conflates the greetings of Gabriel and Elizabeth to her (Luke 1:28, 42). It was widely used from the fifth century, without the closing phrase, "pray for us sinners now and at the hour of our death", which was first added in the fifteenth century, and included in the Roman Breviary by Pius V in 1568. The English Reformers criticized this invocation and similar forms of prayer, because they believed that it threatened the unique mediation of

Jesus Christ. Confronted with exaggerated devotion, stemming from excessive exaltation of Mary's role and powers alongside Christ's, they rejected the "Romish doctrine of . . . the Invocation of Saints" as "grounded upon no warranty of Scripture, but rather repugnant to the Word of God" (Article XXII). The Council of Trent affirmed that seeking the saints' assistance to obtain favours from God is "good and useful": such requests are made "through his Son our Lord Jesus Christ, who is our sole Redeemer and Saviour" (DS 1821). The Second Vatican Council endorsed the continued practice of believers asking Mary to pray for them, emphasising that "Mary's maternal role towards the human race in no way obscures or diminishes the unique mediation of Christ, but rather shows its power . . . in no way does it hinder the direct union of believers with Christ, but rather fosters it" (*Lumen Gentium* 60). Therefore the Roman Catholic Church continues to promote devotion to Mary, while reproving those who either exaggerate or minimize Mary's role (*Marialis Cultus* 31). With this background in mind, we seek a theologically grounded way to draw more closely together in the life of prayer in communion with Christ and his saints.

68 The Scriptures teach that "there is also one mediator between God and humankind, Christ Jesus, himself human, who gave himself as a ransom for all"
(1 Timothy 2:5–6). As noted earlier, on the basis of
this teaching "we reject any interpretation of the role
of Mary which obscures this affirmation" (*Authority
II*, 30). It is also true, however, that all ministries of
the Church, especially those of Word and sacrament,
mediate the grace of God through human beings.
These ministries do not compete with the unique
mediation of Christ, but rather serve it and have their
source within it. In particular, the prayer of the
Church does not stand alongside or in place of the
intercession of Christ, but is made through him, our
Advocate and Mediator (cf. Romans 8:34, Hebrews
7:25, 12:24, 1 John 2:1). It finds both its possibility
and practice in and through the Holy Spirit, the
other Advocate sent according to Christ's promise
(cf. John 14:16–17). Hence asking our brothers and
sisters, on earth and in heaven, to pray for us, does
not contest the unique mediatory work of Christ,
but is rather a means by which, in and through the
Spirit, its power may be displayed.

69 In our praying as Christians we address our petitions to God our heavenly Father, in and through Jesus Christ, as the Holy Spirit moves and enables us. All such invocation takes place within the communion which is God's being and gift. In the life of prayer we invoke the name of Christ in solidarity with the whole Church, assisted by the prayers of brothers and sisters of every time and place. As ARCIC has expressed it previously, "The believer's pilgrimage of faith is lived out with the mutual support of all the people of God. In Christ all the faithful, both living and departed, are bound together in a communion of prayer" (*Salvation and the Church* (1987), 22). In the experience of this communion of prayer, believers are aware of their continued fellowship with their sisters and brothers who have 'fallen asleep', the 'great cloud of witnesses' who surround us as we run the race of faith. For some, this intuition means sensing their friends' presence; for some it may mean pondering the issues of life with those who have gone before them in faith. Such intuitive experience affirms our solidarity in Christ with Christians of every time and place, not least with the woman through whom he became "like us in all things except sin" (Hebrews 4:15).

70 The Scriptures invite Christians to ask their brothers and sisters to pray for them, in and through Christ (cf. James 5:13–15). Those who are now 'with Christ', untrammelled by sin, share the unceasing prayer and praise which characterizes the life of heaven (e.g. Revelation 5:9–14, 7:9–12, 8:3–4). In the light of these testimonies, many Christians have found that requests for assistance in prayer can rightly and effectively be made to those members of the communion of saints distinguished by their holy living (cf. James 5:16–18). It is in this sense that we affirm that asking the saints to pray for us is not to be excluded as unscriptural, though it is not directly taught by the scriptures to be a required element of life in Christ. Further, we agree that the way such assistance is sought must not obscure believers' direct access to God our heavenly Father, who delights to give good gifts to his children (Matthew 7:11). When, in the Spirit and through Christ, believers address their prayers to God, they are assisted by the prayers of other believers, especially of those who are truly alive in Christ and freed from sin. We note that liturgical forms of prayer are addressed to God: they do not address prayer 'to' the saints, but rather ask them to 'pray for us'. However, in this and other instances, any concept of invocation which blurs the trinitarian economy of grace and hope is to be rejected, as not consonant with Scripture or the ancient common traditions.

The Distinctive Ministry of Mary

71 Among all the saints, Mary takes her place as *Theotókos*: alive in Christ, she abides with the one she bore, still 'highly favoured' in the communion of grace and hope, the exemplar of redeemed humanity, an icon of the Church. Consequently she is believed to exercise a distinctive ministry of assisting others through her active prayer. Many Christians reading the Cana account continue to hear Mary instruct them, "Do whatever he tells you", and are confident that she draws the attention of her son to their needs: "they have no wine" (John 2:1–12). Many experience a sense of empathy and solidarity with Mary, especially at key points when the account of her life echoes theirs, for example the acceptance of vocation, the scandal of her pregnancy, the improvised surroundings of her labour, giving birth, and fleeing as a refugee. Portrayals of Mary standing at the foot of the cross, and the traditional portrayal of her receiving the crucified body of Jesus (the *Pietà*), evoke the particular suffering of a mother at the death of her child. Anglicans and Roman Catholics alike are drawn to the mother of Christ, as a figure of tenderness and compassion.

72 The motherly role of Mary, first affirmed in the gospel accounts of her relationship to Jesus, has been developed in a variety of ways. Christian believers acknowledge Mary to be the mother of God incarnate. As they ponder our Saviour's dying word to the beloved disciple, "behold your mother" (John 19:27) they may hear an invitation to hold Mary dear as 'mother of the faithful': she will care for them as she cared for her son in his hour of need. Hearing Eve called "the mother of all living" (Genesis 3:20), they may come to see Mary as mother of the new humanity, active in her ministry of pointing all people to Christ, seeking the welfare of all the living. We are agreed that, while caution is needed in the use of such imagery, it is fitting to apply it to Mary, as a way of honouring her distinctive relationship to her son, and the efficacy in her of his redeeming work.

73 Many Christians find that giving devotional expression to their appreciation for this ministry of Mary enriches their worship of God. Authentic popular devotion to Mary, which by its nature displays a wide individual, regional, and cultural diversity, is to be respected. The crowds gathering at some places where Mary is believed to have appeared suggest

that such apparitions are an important part of this devotion and provide spiritual comfort. There is need for careful discernment in assessing the spiritual value of any alleged apparition. This has been emphasized in a recent Roman Catholic commentary.

> Private revelation . . . can be a genuine help in understanding the Gospel and living it better at a particular moment in time; therefore it should not be disregarded. It is a help which is offered, but which one is not obliged to use . . . The criterion for the truth and value of a private revelation is therefore its orientation to Christ himself. When it leads us away from him, when it becomes independent of him or even presents itself as another and better plan of salvation, more important than the Gospel, then it certainly does not come from the Holy Spirit (*Congregation for the Doctrine of the Faith, "Theological Commentary on the Message of Fatima", June 26, 2000*).

We are agreed that, within the constraints set down in this teaching to ensure that the honour paid to Christ remains pre-eminent, such private devotion is acceptable, though never required of believers.

74 When Mary was first acknowledged as mother of the Lord by Elizabeth, she responded by praising God and proclaiming his justice for the poor in her *Magnificat* (Luke 1:46–55). In Mary's response we can see an attitude of poverty towards God that reflects the divine commitment and preference for the poor. In her powerlessness she is exalted by God's favour. Although the witness of her obedience and acceptance of God's will has sometimes been used to encourage passivity and impose servitude on women, it is rightly seen as a radical commitment to God who has mercy on his servant, lifts up the lowly and brings down the mighty. Issues of justice for women and the empowerment of the oppressed have arisen from daily reflection on Mary's remarkable song. Inspired by her words, communities of women and men in various cultures have committed themselves to work with the poor and the excluded. Only when joy is joined with justice and peace do we rightly share in the economy of hope and grace which Mary proclaims and embodies.

75 Affirming together unambiguously Christ's unique mediation, which bears fruit in the life of the Church, we do not consider the practice of asking Mary and the saints to pray for us as communion

dividing. Since obstacles of the past have been removed by clarification of doctrine, by liturgical reform and practical norms in keeping with it, we believe that there is no continuing theological reason for ecclesial division on these matters.

CONCLUSION

76 Our study, which opens with a careful ecclesial and ecumenical reading of the Scriptures, in the light of the ancient common traditions, has illuminated in a new way the place of Mary in the economy of hope and grace. We together re-affirm the agreements reached previously by ARCIC, in *Authority in the Church* II.30:

- that any interpretation of the role of Mary must not obscure the unique mediation of Christ;

- that any consideration of Mary must be linked with the doctrines of Christ and the Church;

- that we recognize the Blessed Virgin Mary as the *Theotókos*, the mother of God incarnate, and so observe her festivals and accord her honour among the saints;

- that Mary was prepared by grace to be the mother of our Redeemer, by whom she herself was redeemed and received into glory;

- that we recognize Mary as a model of holiness, faith, and obedience for all Christians; and

- that Mary can be seen as a prophetic figure of the Church.

We believe that the present statement significantly deepens and extends these agreements, setting them within a comprehensive study of doctrine and devotion associated with Mary.

77 We are convinced that any attempt to come to a reconciled understanding of these matters must begin by listening to God's word in the Scriptures. Therefore our common statement commences with a careful exploration of the rich New Testament witness to

Mary, in the light of overall themes and patterns in the Scriptures as a whole.

- This study has led us to the conclusion that it is impossible to be faithful to Scripture without giving due attention to the person of Mary (paras 6–30).

- In recalling together the ancient common traditions, we have discerned afresh the central importance of the *Theotókos* in the Christological controversies, and the Fathers' use of biblical images to interpret and celebrate Mary's place in the plan of salvation (paras 31–40).

- We have reviewed the growth of devotion to Mary in the medieval centuries, and the theological controversies associated with them. We have seen how some excesses in late medieval devotion, and reactions against them by the Reformers, contributed to the breach of communion between us, following which attitudes toward Mary took divergent paths (paras 41–6).

- We have also noted evidence of subsequent developments in both our Communions, which opened the way for a re-reception of the place of Mary in the faith and life of the Church (paras 47–51).

- This growing convergence has also allowed us to approach in a fresh way the questions about Mary which our two Communions have set before us. In doing so, we have framed our work within the pattern of grace and hope which we discover in Scripture—"predestined . . . called . . . justified . . . glorified" (Romans 8:30) (paras 52–7).

Advances in Agreement

78 As a result of our study, the Commission offers the following agreements, which we believe significantly advance our consensus regarding Mary. We affirm together

- the teaching that God has taken the Blessed Virgin Mary in the fullness of her person into his glory as consonant with

Scripture, and only to be understood in the light of Scripture (para. 58);

- that in view of her vocation to be the mother of the Holy One, Christ's redeeming work reached 'back' in Mary to the depths of her being and to her earliest beginnings (para. 59);

- that the teaching about Mary in the two definitions of the Assumption and the Immaculate Conception, understood within the biblical pattern of the economy of hope and grace, can be said to be consonant with the teaching of the Scriptures and the ancient common traditions (para. 60);

- that this agreement, when accepted by our two Communions, would place the questions about authority which arise from the two definitions of 1854 and 1950 in a new ecumenical context (paras 61–3);

- that Mary has a continuing ministry which serves the ministry of Christ, our unique

mediator, that Mary and the Saints pray
for the whole Church and that the practice of asking Mary and the saints to pray
for us is not communion-dividing (paras
64–75).

79 We agree that doctrines and devotions which are
contrary to Scripture cannot be said to be revealed
by God nor to be the teaching of the Church. We
agree that doctrine and devotion which focuses on
Mary, including claims to 'private revelations', must
be moderated by carefully expressed norms which
ensure the unique and central place of Jesus Christ in
the life of the Church, and that Christ alone, together
with the Father and the Holy Spirit, is to be wor-
shipped in the Church.

80 Our statement has sought not to clear away all possible problems, but to deepen our common understanding to the point where remaining diversities of
devotional practice may be received as the varied
work of the Spirit amongst all the people of God. We
believe that the agreement we have here outlined is
itself the product of a re-reception by Anglicans and
Roman Catholics of doctrine about Mary and that it
points to the possibility of further reconciliation, in

which issues concerning doctrine and devotion to Mary need no longer be seen as communion-dividing, or an obstacle in a new stage of our growth into visible *koinonia*. This agreed statement is now offered to our respective authorities. It may also in itself prove a valuable study of the teaching of the Scriptures and the ancient common traditions about the Blessed Virgin Mary, the Mother of God incarnate. Our hope is that, as we share in the one Spirit by which Mary was prepared and sanctified for her unique vocation, we may together participate with her and all the saints in the unending praise of God.

✤ Study Guide

INTRODUCTION

This study guide has been prepared with the intention of addressing some of the main themes of the Mary statement, which reflect principal aspects of the understanding of Mary in the life of the Church: as Mother of God; as a model of discipleship; as reflecting the pattern of God's saving work; as one who was the recipient of grace from the very beginning of her existence; as one taken into God's glory; as a mother to the Church. These will be familiar territory for those for whom Mary is an important part of their faith; probably quite a new landscape for those for whom devotion to Mary has not been part of their own spiritual journey.

The studies are designed in six sections, so that they can be used as a series of weekly sessions, perhaps in Lent, in May, or at another time of year. But they may also serve as a resource for personal study and reflection. We particularly hope that they might be used by Anglicans and Catholics studying together.

Each section begins with a reflection on the topic for the session: providing a framework for the subject being addressed, and introducing ARCIC's treatment of it in the Mary statement. There follow two passages for study. One is from the Mary statement itself – a paragraph or two that seem to us to crystallise the thinking of the Commission, and a second passage from the Scriptures, which illuminates the discussion in the statement, and which draws us back to the scriptural foundations of our faith.

We also offer four questions for personal reflection or discussion: some of these have a deliberate focus on the lives of worshipping Anglican and Roman Catholic congregations.

Finally, we close each section by including two prayers drawn from our traditions, which pick up on themes addressed in that section. While assisting the study of the matter being reflected upon, they could also be used as opening and closing prayers for joint study sessions. In two cases, these prayers are supplemented by devotions which derive from our common tradition before the Reformation.

Week One

The Mother of God

Background reading:
MGHC §1–7, 12–30, 31–4

Christian belief is grounded in history—not solely
   historical events, although there is, Christians believe,
   a sure foundation of historical events. The history
   pondered by the believer is salvation history, the
   story of God's redeeming action in the history of the
   world. It is within this framework—of historical
   events which carry within them the history of salvation—that Christians look to a young Jewish
   woman, living in Judaea at the time of the Roman
   occupation, who was called by God to give birth to

a child. Christians recognise in that child the Son of God, the Incarnate Word, entering the world to encompass its redemption by his death and resurrection.

ARCIC's study of Mary therefore begins with the story of Mary as it has been recorded in the New Testament (§12–29), and principally, in the Gospels. Here is the story of the mother of Jesus, the announcement of the coming birth of her son, and the account of his birth, as told by Matthew (§12, 13, 18), and then by Luke (§14–17, 18); the story of the family of Jesus (§19–20); events recorded about Mary and Jesus in John's Gospel (§22–7); and the account of Mary and the other disciples waiting for the coming of the Holy Spirit in Acts (§21).

When Anglicans and Catholics ponder the story of Mary and reflect upon her role in the teaching and life of the Church, we are looking at Mary's place in salvation history, to her place in God's revelation. We turn first to the Scriptures, because, as ARCIC noted, "[w]e remain convinced that the holy Scriptures, as the Word of God written, bear normative witness to God's plan of salvation" (§6). Furthermore, we turn to the Scriptures together, mindful that for over four centuries, tragically, we have read and interpreted the Scriptures in a context of separation. When the members of ARCIC read the Scriptures together, enquiring into the place of Mary, they noted that it was "impossible to be faithful to Scripture without giving due attention to the person of Mary" (§77; cf §6). What they discovered was "more than just a few tantalising glimpses into the life of a great saint. We have found ourselves meditating with wonder and gratitude on the whole sweep of salvation history: creation, election, the Incarnation, passion, and resurrection of Christ, the gift of the Spirit in the Church, and the final vision of eternal life for all God's people in the new creation" (§6).

Anglicans and Catholics also turn to the early Church, notably the patristic writings and the councils and creeds of the first five centuries, since those early Christians had also meditated upon the place of Mary in salvation history. The Mary statement (§31–4) stresses the central importance of the early Church's understanding of Mary as the Mother of God the Word Incarnate, the 'God-bearer' (*Theotókos*). This title was given to Mary by the Christian teachers and councils of the fifth century to demonstrate the theological reality of the fact that her son, the historical Jesus, was also none other than God Incarnate. In this title, as in the Scriptures,

Mary is always seen in relation to Christ. Reflection on Mary in the early Church was not an end in itself, but rather, a way of reflecting on Christ as fully human (born of Mary; §32) and fully divine (conceived by the Holy Spirit; §33).

Passages for Study

From the Bible: Luke 1:39–2:20
From the Mary statement: §30

Questions for discussion:

Through the ages, the image of a human being, Mary, carrying within her the Incarnate Son of God, has stirred the Christian imagination. The early Church writer Eusebius speaks of how Mary, for nine months, "entertained within the closet of her flesh the hope of all the ends of the earth". The Anglican poet John Donne grapples with the paradox of Mary as her "maker's maker"; she is the blessed one "whose womb was a strange heaven, for there God clothed himself, and grew ..."

- What does the title 'Mother of God' mean to you? Is it helpful in drawing attention to what Christians believe about the identity of Jesus?

- When you reflect on the role of Mary in the Incarnation, what implications might be drawn from it in terms of your life of faith as a disciple of Jesus Christ?

- The Mary document notes that it is "impossible to be faithful to Scripture without giving due attention to the person of Mary". Does the consideration of Mary in the Scriptures in the ARCIC statement offer any new insights for you, or raise any questions?

- ARCIC states in several places that Mary should always be seen and understood in relation to Christ (cf §2, 15, 51). The title 'Mother of God' stresses that relationship and offers a profound insight into the role of Mary in salvation history. Since Anglicans and Catholics alike understand Mary in this way, what might be some of the implications for the life of our churches?

PRAYERS AND REFLECTION:

A fifteenth-century anonymous carol speaks of Mary as a Rose, giving birth to Christ:

There is no rose of sych vertu
As is the rose that bare Jesu,
Alleluia.

For in this rose contained was
Heaven and earth in lytle space,
Res miranda.
By that rose we may well see

That He is God in persons three,
Pares forma.

The aungels sungen the shepherds to:
Gloria in excelsis Deo,
Gaudeamus.

Leave we all this wearldly mirth,
And follow we this joyful birth,
Transeamus.

Alleluia, res miranda,
Pares forma, gaudeamus,
Transeamus.[1]

❧

Crown him the virgin's Son,
the God incarnate born,
whose arm those crimson trophies won
which now his brow adorn:
fruit of the mystic rose,
as of that rose the stem;
the root whence mercy ever flows,
the babe of Bethlehem.

(from the hymn, "Crown him with many crowns",
additional verses by Godfrey Thring, 1874)

---

1 *Res Miranda*—a miraculous thing; *pares forma*—in the form of equal parts;
 gaudeamus—let us rejoice; *transeamus*—we pass away.

Let us pray in the name of Jesus, born of a virgin and
   Son of God:

Father, source of light in every age,

the virgin conceived and bore your Son who is called
   Wonderful God, Prince of Peace.

May her prayer, the gift of a mother's love, be your
   people's joy through all ages.

May her response, born of a humble heart, draw your
   Spirit to rest on your people.

Grant this through Christ our Lord. Amen.

(Alternative Opening Prayer for the Feast of Mary,
Mother of God; Catholic Sacramentary)

Week Two

A Pattern of Discipleship, Model of the Church

Background reading:
MGHC preface, §5, 8–9, 51

By her willingness to be caught up into the plan of
   God, Mary provides us with a model of the response
   which all disciples are called to give to the call of
   God in Jesus Christ. In their preface to the Mary
   statement, ARCIC's Co-Chairs wrote: "Mary, the
   mother of our Lord Jesus Christ, stands before us as
   an exemplar of faithful obedience", and her *fiat*—
   "Be it done unto to me according to your word"
   (Luke 1:38)—is "the grace-filled response each of us

is called to make to God, both personally and communally, as the Church, the body of Christ".

The Mary statement turns repeatedly to Mary's encounter with the angel Gabriel, and her receptivity to what is being asked of her (Luke 1:26–38), reflecting at one and the same time on the distinctiveness of her calling and on her response as a pattern for Christian discipleship. In §5, the text introduces a framework of dialogue, drawing on 2 Corinthians 1:19–20, which was developed in ARCIC's 1999 Agreed Statement *The Gift of Authority*. In this framework, God's actions in the world (in Christ) are characterized as an unambiguous 'Yes', an affirmation and fulfilment of God's covenant of love with humanity. God's 'Yes' calls forth a welcoming human response—our 'Amen'.

Within this framework, Mary's *fiat*—her willing response to Gabriel's message—can be seen as epitomising the Christian's 'Amen' to God's call and invitation. It is God's grace which enabled Mary's positive response, yet that response was given in faith and freedom, expressing her readiness "to let everything in her life happen according to God's word" (§20). Mary's calling was distinctive and unique: "The Incarnation and all that it entailed, including the passion, death and resurrection of Christ and the birth of the Church, came about by way of Mary's freely uttered *fiat*". As such, Mary's graced response "can be seen as the supreme instance of a believer's 'Amen' in response to the 'Yes' of God" (§5). At the same time, her response is "a model for every disciple and for the life of the Church" (§64): "When Christians join in Mary's 'Amen' to the 'Yes' of God in Christ, they commit themselves to an obedient response to the Word of God, which leads to a life of prayer and service. Like Mary, they not only magnify the Lord with their lips: they commit themselves to serve God's justice with their lives (*cf* Luke 1:46–55)" (§5).

The Mary statement also draws on St John's account of the wedding at Cana (2:1–12) in presenting Mary as embodying the pattern of Christian discipleship (§23–5). The Commission sees in this narrative a transition in the relationship between Jesus and Mary; while the beginning of the story places Jesus within the family of his mother, at the end of the story, Mary is presented as "part of the 'company of Jesus', his disciple" (§25). The key turning point is when Mary addresses the servants and tells them to "do what whatever he tells you" (John 2:5), words which reflect "the Church's understanding of the role of Mary: to help the disciples come to her son, Jesus Christ" (§25).

The Mary statement expands on the understanding of God's call set forth in the Scriptures in §8–9 and in §51. All Christians are invited to allow God to enter their lives and respond to God's call, faithful to the covenant which God has made with us in Christ. Mary "received the Word in her heart and in her body, and brought it forth into the world" (§51). So too is the community of believers called to find room for the Lord in their hearts, and to make his love known to the world.

Just as ARCIC insists that Mary should be seen always in relation to Christ, so too is she inseparably linked to the Church, as a model of the holiness, obedience and prophetic proclamation to which the Church is called. In this way, Mary becomes the model not only for the individual believer's response to God, but also the model for the way in which the Church as a whole has to be responsive to God's will, and show him forth to the world. Mary embodies not only the pattern of discipleship, but in herself becomes a figure representative of the Church.

PASSAGES FOR STUDY
From the Bible: Luke 1:26–38
From the Mary statement: §5, 51

Questions for discussion:

- How far does the model of Mary's response to God offer us a model for our own response to God's invitation?

- How is Mary's vocation like our own, and how is it different and unique?

- In icons of Mary with the child Jesus, Mary is often shown pointing to the Christ child. How can we point to the Living Word of God in our own lives, and in the lives of our churches?

- In the Song of Mary, the *Magnificat*, which is used in the worship of both Anglicans and Roman Catholics, Mary celebrates the action of God in the world. How far does the *Magnificat* set forth an agenda for the common life of our churches in their different localities?

Prayers and Reflection:

Father in Heaven, by whose grace the virgin mother of your incarnate Son was blessed in bearing him, but still more blessed in keeping your word: grant to us who honour the exaltation of her lowliness to follow the example of her devotion to your will: through the same Jesus Christ our Lord, who lives and reigns with you and the Holy Spirit, one God, for ever and ever. Amen.

(The Collect for the Feast of the Visitation
from the Book of Common Prayer
for the Episcopal Church (USA), adapted)

Father, all-powerful God, your eternal Word took flesh on our earth when the Virgin Mary placed her life at the service of your plan. Lift our minds in watchful hope to hear the voice which announces his glory and open our minds to receive the Spirit who prepares us for his coming. We ask this through Christ our Lord.

(Alternative Opening Prayer,
4th Sunday of Advent;
Catholic Sacramentary)

Week Three

The Pattern of Salvation

Background reading:
MGHC §8–11, 19-20, 52–7

Over the centuries, as Christians have reflected on
Mary's life and discipleship, a body of teaching has
developed as Christians have sought to understand
how God's grace had been at work in one called to
such a significant vocation as being the mother of the
Messiah. In particular, two doctrines have become
highly significant to Catholic faith—the doctrine of
the Immaculate Conception, which refers to the
conception of Mary as the child of Anna and

Joachim,[2] and the Assumption, which refers to Mary's entry, body and soul, into heavenly glory. These two teachings are the focus of further studies.

In order to understand these doctrines, ARCIC sought to place them within the way in which God works for the salvation of all humanity. "We have sought to understand Mary's person and role in the history of salvation and the life of the Church in the light of a theology of divine grace and hope" (§4). In particular, ARCIC turned to a passage in the writings of St Paul, in which he sets out the pattern of God's intervention in human life (Romans 8:28, §10, 52, 53):

And those whom he predestined he also called; and those whom he called he also justified; and those whom he justified he also glorified.

(Romans 8:30)

In other words, God begins his work in all disciples from eternity, and for eternity. From this perspective, Mary becomes the pattern of how God works to bring every disciple of Jesus into the fullness of life which is his will for us.

---

2 These are the names by which Mary's parents have become known in Christian tradition. There is no direct historical evidence for these names, but they are the only names known to be ascribed to Mary's mother and father, and both are recognised as saints in their own right.

The Mary statement sets out how the pattern of God's choosing and calling is reflected right across the Scriptures. It also points to a biblical pattern of God glorifying those who have faithfully witnessed to God's redeeming work in history. These themes will be developed in Weeks 4 and 5 respectively.

It is interesting to note that ARCIC often addresses the question of God's pattern of salvation from its end point, rather than its beginning. The Commission begins with the fact that God has revealed the future destiny of his people in Christ. "For Paul especially, what it means to be fully human can only be understood rightly when it is viewed in the light of what we are to become in Christ" (§52). It is this purpose and goal of God's acts of redemption which make sense of the Christian vocation to live a life of holiness, and of God's enabling acts of grace in the life of the believer (§53).

For many protestant Christians, one of their chief concerns about devotion to Mary is that she appears to be given almost divine status in some Catholic devotion; Mary seems to be treated as if she is not a human being subject to the same need of salvation as the rest of humanity. This, of course, is not true to Catholic teaching. By identifying the pattern of salvation for all humanity in Romans, and showing how Mary conforms to that pattern, ARCIC hopes to emphasise Mary's solidarity as a redeemed believer with all of the family of Christ.

PASSAGES FOR STUDY
From the Bible: Romans 8:18–35
From the Mary statement: §10, 53

QUESTIONS FOR DISCUSSION

- How does what Paul teaches in chapter 8 of the Letter to the Romans apply to Mary's experience?
- How does the example of Mary's journey of faith help you to understand how God works in the lives of all believers?
- How are we like Mary as disciples? How are we unlike?
- How far can our churches celebrate together the work of God in Mary as a pattern for how God works in us?

PRAYERS AND REFLECTION:
" ... we do well always and everywhere to give you thanks, and to praise you for your gifts as we contemplate your saints in glory. In celebrating the memory of the Blessed Virgin Mary, it is our special joy to echo

her song of thanksgiving. What wonders you have worked throughout the world. All generations have shared the greatness of your love."

(Preface, Common of the Blessed Virgin Mary,
Catholic Sacramentary)

Mighty God,
by whose grace Elizabeth rejoiced with Mary and greeted her as the mother of the Lord: look with favour on your lowly servants that, with Mary, we may magnify your holy name and rejoice to acclaim her Son our Saviour, who is alive and reigns with you and the Holy Spirit, ever one God, world without end. Amen.

(Collect for the Feast of the Visitation, Common Worship:
Services and Prayers for the Church of England)

Week Four

God's Grace

Background reading:
MGHC §35–9, 52–5, 59

Given that Mary was called by God to be the mother
of the Saviour, and bear him who is fully human and
fully divine in her womb for nine months,
Christians have long pondered in what way Mary
was prepared in advance for this vocation and
responsibility. In 1854, Pope Pius IX defined the
dogma of the Immaculate Conception of Mary,
binding Roman Catholics to the belief that "the
most blessed Virgin Mary was, from the first
moment of her conception, by a singular grace and

privilege of almighty God and in view of the merits of Christ Jesus the Saviour of the human race, preserved immune from all stain of original sin". According to the definition, like every human being, Mary can only be saved through Christ. But the dogma suggests that the redeeming grace won by Christ on the Cross was already operative in Mary's life even from the time of her conception.

When the angel Gabriel addressed Mary (Luke 1:28), she was called the Lord's "favoured one" (literally, 'one who has been and remains endowed with grace'), suggesting that Mary had already been sanctified by divine grace with a view to her calling (§16). The implications of this 'prevenient grace' in Mary's life for her discipleship was something which was explored from the earliest centuries of Christian faith. This history is recounted in the Agreed Statement in §35–9; most notable here is the strong affirmation already in the fifth century of the view that "Mary was filled with grace from her origin in anticipation of her unique vocation as Mother of the Lord" and the emergence in the sixth century of the title *panaghia* ('all-holy') being applied to Mary (§38).

In reflecting on the dogma of the Immaculate Conception in the light of the Scriptures and ancient common traditions, ARCIC turned its attention once again to the pattern of God's redemptive work in all human beings set out in Chapter 8 of Paul's letter to the Romans. In this instance, it is the first part of that pattern which is particularly relevant: "for those whom he foreknew he also predestined to be conformed to the image of his Son ... And those whom he predestined he also called ...". The Agreed Statement noted that Christians "have discerned a similar pattern in the one who would receive the Word in her heart and in her body, be overshadowed by the Spirit and give birth to the Son of God" (§11). Furthermore, the Scriptures bear witness to God's providential care for those who have been called even before their birth (Psalm 139:13–18) and God's grace "preceding the specific calling of particular persons, even from their conception" (§55). The most important example given is that of Jeremiah, to whom God says: "Before I formed you in the womb I knew you, and before you were born I consecrated you" (1:5). Of Mary, ARCIC is able to affirm that "the glorious grace of God filled her life from the beginning", and that she is indeed "the prototype of the hope of grace for humankind as a whole" (§55).

The Mary document's argument, initially introduced in §10–11 and then further developed in §54–5, culminates in §59:

In view of her vocation to be the mother of the Holy One (Luke 1:35), we can affirm together that Christ's redeeming work reached 'back' in Mary to the depths of her being, and to her earliest beginnings. This is not contrary to the teaching of Scripture, and can only be understood in the light of Scripture. Roman Catholics can recognize in this what is affirmed by the dogma—namely preserved from all stain of original sin and 'from the first moment of her conception'.

Passages for Study

From the Bible: Luke 1:28; Psalm 139:13–18; Jeremiah 1:4–5

From the Mary statement: §54–5, 59

Questions for Discussion:

- MGHC draws out the meaning of Mary's 'sinlessness' by noting that "it is not so much that Mary lacks something which other human beings 'have', namely sin, but that the glorious grace of God filled her life from the beginning". This grace reflects the efficacy of Christ's atoning sacrifice for one who preceded him in time (cf §59). While we struggle with sin, we too know the experience of God's grace, which reaches to the depths of our being.

How far can you describe your discipleship as an experience of grace, and compare your experience with that of Mary?

- Do you have a sense of having been graced by God for a particular vocation, and if so, is Mary's free acceptance of God's call a source of hope for you? If not, might it be?

- The dogma of the Immaculate Conception of Mary is an essential part of the faith of the Roman Catholic Church. What does the concept of Mary's 'sinlessness' add to our understanding of who Jesus was?

- Many Anglicans will find this dogma problematic. What are the strengths and weaknesses of ARCIC's arguments in the Mary statement?

PRAYERS AND REFLECTION:

And now we give you thanks for the obedience of your servant Mary, who by your grace answered your call to be the mother of your Son. With all generations we call her blessed, and with her we rejoice in the greatness of your salvation.

(Proper Preface for Our Lady, A Prayer Book for Australia)

Father, you prepared the Virgin Mary to be the worthy mother of your Son. You let her share beforehand in the salvation Christ would bring by his death, and kept her sinless from the first moment of her conception. Help us by her prayers to live in your presence without sin. We ask this through our Lord Jesus Christ, your Son, who lives and reigns with you and the Holy Spirit, one God, for ever and ever.

(Opening Prayer, Feast of the Immaculate Conception, Catholic Sacramentary)

Week Five

Hope in Christ

Background reading:
§40, 56–8, 60–3, 76–80

When Anglicans and Roman Catholics profess the Apostles' or Nicaeo-Constantinopolitan Creed, we express our belief in "the resurrection of the body", our hope that the whole of our personalities—body and soul—will be redeemed and brought into God's presence for eternity. This hope, grounded in the Scriptures and in the ancient common tradition, provides a context for understanding the Catholic dogma of the Assumption of Mary defined in 1950 by Pope Pius XII. The dogma does not indicate how Mary's life ended and it uses about her neither the language of death and resurrection nor that of ascension (cf §58). Rather, it suggests that Christ shares with his mother his victory over death, by defining that Mary, "having completed the course of her earthly life, was assumed body and soul into heavenly glory".

The history of this belief within the Church is recounted in the Mary statement in §40. In the East, a feast of Mary's 'falling asleep' or 'dormition' dates from the end of the sixth century; the term 'dormition' implies Mary's death but does not exclude her being taken into heaven. In the West "the term used was 'assumption', which emphasized her being taken into heaven but did not exclude the possibility of her dying". Belief in Mary's assumption was grounded in the recognition of Mary's dignity as Mother of God, "coupled with the conviction that she who had borne Life should be associated to her Son's victory over death, and with the glorification of his Body, the Church" (§40).

In reflecting on the teaching that at the end of her life Mary was taken into God's presence, the Mary document again looks to the pattern of God's saving work in Romans 8:28-30: foreknew-predestined-called-justified-glorified. In §56, the text draws attention to a scriptural pattern of those who faithfully follow God's purposes being welcomed into the presence of God at the end of their lives (Elijah, Enoch, Stephen). While noting that there is no direct testimony in the Scriptures regarding the end of Mary's life, the text reflects on Mary as the one who bore God incarnate in her womb, noting that "her bodily intimacy with her son was all of a piece with her faithful following of him, and her maternal participation in his victorious self-giving (Luke 2:35)". Here the text echoes the opening paragraph, which introduces Mary as "the one who, of all believers, is closest to our Lord and Saviour Jesus Christ" (§1). This provides a context for appreciating anew the tradition regarding the end of Mary's life: "When Christians from East and West through the generations have pondered God's work in Mary, they have discerned in faith ... that it is fitting that the Lord gathered her wholly to himself" (§57).

In drawing various strands of reflection together, the Mary statement concludes that Mary's destiny thus understood can be seen as a type of the Church, a sign of hope in the glorification which is God's desire for us all. With regard to the dogma of the Assumption of Mary, the text concludes:

we can affirm together the teaching that God has taken the Blessed Virgin Mary in the fullness of her person into his glory as consonant with Scripture and that it can, indeed, only be understood in the light of Scripture. Roman Catholics can recognize that this teaching about Mary is contained in the dogma. (§58)

The Mary document does not claim to resolve entirely the differences between Anglicans and Catholics regarding the two Marian dogmas, for the positive affirmations in §58–9 and reiterated in the Conclusion (§78) pertain to the Marian content of the dogmas, not the authority by which they were defined. Nonetheless, ARCIC felt confident in proposing that if the arguments laid forth in the Mary document were accepted by the Anglican Communion and the Catholic Church, this "would place the questions about authority which arise from the two definitions of 1854 and 1950 in a new ecumenical context" (§78; cf §60–3).

PASSAGES FOR STUDY
From the Bible: Philippians 1.3–11
From the Mary statement: §56–8

QUESTIONS FOR DISCUSSION:

- Reflecting on the scriptural pattern of those at the end of their lives being brought into the glory of God, how would you express the Christian hope?

- In Philippians, Paul speaks of God bringing his work of redemption to completion in people's lives. How does the destiny of Mary compare with the work of God in our own lives?

- Given that Anglicans and Roman Catholics share the same hope for a future lived in the presence of God's glory, how might belief in Mary's assumption be a strengthening of our own hope for ourselves and for humanity?

- How is this conviction that Mary is, of all believers, closest to Jesus Christ reflected in the life of your church? How might it be appropriately reflected in the spiritual life of believers?

PRAYERS AND REFLECTION:

Let us pray (that with the help of Mary's prayers we too may reach our heavenly home): Father in heaven, all creation rightly gives you praise, for all life and all holiness come from you. In the plan of your wisdom she who bore the Christ in her womb was raised body and soul in glory to be with him in heaven. May we follow her example in reflecting your holi-

ness and join in her hymn of endless life and praise.
We ask this through Christ our Lord.

(Alternative Opening Prayer, Feast of the Assumption,
Catholic Sacramentary)

Almighty and everlasting God, who stooped to raise
fallen humanity through the child-bearing of
blessed Mary: grant that we, who have seen your
glory revealed in human nature and your love made
perfect in our weakness, may daily be renewed in
your image and conformed to the pattern of your
Son, Jesus Christ our Lord, who is alive and reigns
with you and the Holy Spirit, ever one God, world
without end. Amen.

(Collect for the Feast of the Nativity of Mary,
Common Worship: Services and Prayers for
the Church of England)

Week Six

A Mother for the Church

Background reading:
MGHC §49–50, 64–75

When Jesus was challenged about the way he spoke of
some of the great Jewish forefathers, he said this:
"He is God not of the dead, but of the living" (Mark
12:27). Christians acknowledge as a spiritual reality
that all those redeemed in Christ, even when they
have died, are still in truth alive. And as the life of
God is turned outwards towards the world, so the
life of the saints in heaven are turned with him witnessing the ongoing life of creation from the standpoint of eternity (cf. Hebrews 12:1; Revelation

6.9–11). This means that all the saints have an ongoing ministry of prayer for the Church. Beyond this, in Mary, many Christians through the ages have found that the mother of Jesus offers a particularly attractive figure as someone who, in sharing her son's concerns and suffering (Luke 2:35), cares for the Church and its struggles on earth.

The place of Mary in the devotional life of the Catholic Church has historically been of concern to many Anglicans. In §47–50, the Mary statement looks at ways in which, in recent decades, the Catholic Church and the Anglican Communion have each turned anew to the place of Mary in the Scriptures and in the ancient common tradition. As a result, the Catholic Church since the Second Vatican Council has sought to situate Marian doctrine and devotion within a Christological and ecclesial context. Within Anglican worship, Mary is once again mentioned in eucharistic prayers, and 15 August has been recognized in the liturgical calendar as a principal feast in honour of Mary.

In the final section of the Mary statement (§66–75), the place of Mary in the life of the Church, and in particular, Marian devotion, is addressed. The section begins with a strong affirmation: "We together agree that in understanding Mary as the fullest human example of the life of grace, we are called to reflect on the lessons of her life recorded in Scripture and to join with her as one indeed not dead, but truly alive in Christ" (§65). The text stresses that Marian devotion and the invocation of Mary are not in any way to obscure or diminish the unique mediation of Christ.

All this is focussed in one passage of Scripture, where Mary is presented as mother to the figure who represents all disciples – in John 19:25–7. This passage is discussed in the Agreed Statement in §26 and 27. This passage, when read by Christians down through the centuries, has been understood as inviting all Christians to enter into the intimate family relationship established by Jesus between his mother and his disciple.

To pray with Mary and the saints, and to ask for their prayers, therefore is not to invoke them as an alternative to God, but as family members, who from the standpoint of eternity, can support our journey of faith with their prayers to the same Father who is the source of all good gifts.

The Mary Statement concludes:

Affirming together unambiguously Christ's unique mediation, which bears fruit in the life of the

Church, we do not consider the practice of asking Mary and the saints to pray for us as communion dividing ... we believe that there is no continuing theological reason for ecclesial division on these matters.

Passages for Study:
From the Bible: John 19:25–7
From the Mary statement: §26–7

Questions for Discussion
- In professing belief in the "Communion of Saints" in the Apostles' Creed, both Anglicans and Catholics acknowledge that they are part of the family of God which embraces all his people, both living and departed. How can the realisation of this truth encourage us in our own discipleship?
- How does Mary in particular fit into this larger picture of the ongoing life of the family of God?
- What is helpful in seeing Mary as a Mother to the Church?
- How can Anglicans and Catholics share in this dimension of prayer, both publicly and in their own devotion?

Prayers and Reflection:

The most established prayer to Mary in the life of the
Church is the "Hail, Mary". This is actually a colla-
tion of two biblical texts about Mary: the greeting
of the Archangel Gabriel (Luke 1:28), and the greeting of her cousin Elizabeth in Luke 1:42. It adds a
specific request for Mary's prayers now and at the
moment of greatest human vulnerability.

Hail Mary, full of grace,
The Lord is with thee;
Blessed art thou among women,
And blessed is the fruit of thy womb, Jesus.
Holy Mary, Mother of God,
Pray for us sinners now
And at the hour of our death, Amen.

O higher than the Cherubim.
more glorious than the Seraphim,
Lead their praises, Alleluya!
Thou bearer of the eternal Word,
Most gracious, magnify the Lord,
Alleluya, alleluya, alleluya, alleluya.

(from the hymn, "Ye watchers and ye holy ones",
Athelstan Riley, 1858–1945)

Let us pray [with Mary to the Father, in whose presence she now dwells]: Almighty Father of our Lord
Jesus Christ, you have revealed the beauty of your
power by exalting the lowly virgin of Nazareth and
making her the mother of our Saviour. May the
prayers of this woman bring Jesus to the waiting
world and fill the void of incompletion with the
presence of her child, who lives and reigns with you
and the Holy Spirit, one God, for ever and ever.

(Opening Prayer, Feast of the Annunciation,
Catholic Sacramentary)

CONCLUSION

In the first chapter of the Acts of the Apostles, we are
afforded a glimpse of the early Church at prayer:
Mary, the mother of Jesus, is present in this first
gathering of the disciples after Jesus had ascended to
the Father, joining them in prayer. In every age,
Mary has had her part to play in the life of the
Christian family. She is the guarantor of the human
reality of Jesus: the virginal conception and her title
as 'mother of God' witness eloquently to the nature
of her son, whilst her own discipleship has been seen
as a pattern of every disciple who comes after.

In every generation, Christians have found in Mary,
pre-eminent among the saints, one who is alive in

Christ, and who shares the journey of holiness which every disciple is called to make. They have found in her a companion, a guide and an encouragement; properly not one who replaces her son, but who points to him, inviting a deeper and richer response to Christ's grace, evoking the hope of life with God.

With the Agreed Statement, *Mary: Grace and Hope in Christ*, this heritage of Christian faith has been explored anew. Catholic devotion has been explored in conversation with an Anglican tradition which has not been afraid to interrogate the deposit of faith, and which has, at times, been extremely sceptical of what the Virgin Mary means for Christian faith. Its conclusions, however, are that the pattern of grace and hope extolled in beliefs about Mary are consonant with the pattern of salvation revealed in Holy Scripture; that the place of Mary so understood becomes no reason for division but another cause for the celebration of all the great work that God has done in Christ.

While the Mary document also points to ongoing differences, in particular regarding the authority by which the dogmas were defined, ARCIC members were hopeful that these differences can now be situated within a new context. The conclusion of

Mary: Grace and Hope in Christ (§76-80) sets out what the dialogue commission is convinced it has achieved in the text, expressing ARCIC's conviction that "the present statement significantly deepens and extends" agreement about Mary through the text's comprehensive study of doctrine and devotion associated with her (§76).

We believe that the agreement we have here outlined is itself the product of a re-reception by Anglicans and Roman Catholics of doctrine about Mary and that it points to the possibility of further reconciliation, in which issues concerning doctrine and devotion to Mary need no longer be seen as communion-dividing, or an obstacle in a new stage of our growth into visible *koinonia* ... Our hope is that, as we share in the one Spirit by which Mary was prepared and sanctified for her unique vocation, we may together participate with her and all the saints in the unending praise of God (§80).

In concluding work on this Agreed Statement, ARCIC brought to a culmination the second phase of dialogue between Anglicans and Roman Catholics, a dialogue which has now been going on for forty years. It is our hope that study of this document may not only enrich Christians on their own journey of faith, but also be a cause for discussion and mutual understanding between Christians of different traditions.

As the disciples gathered with Mary in their prayers following Jesus' Ascension into heaven, so may Christians of today find that in meditating on the work of God in this one person, we may all be drawn together in the enrichment of our faith in the God who sets before us the hope of eternal life, and who, in his grace, enables us to enter into its fullness.

It is best to leave the very last words of this study guide to the song recorded in the Scriptures as being Mary's own hymn of praise for all that God does:

My soul magnifies the Lord,
and my spirit rejoices in God my Saviour,
for he has looked with favour
on the lowliness of his servant.
Surely, from now on all generations will call me
  blessed;
for the Mighty One has done great things for me,
and holy is his name.
His mercy is for those who fear him
from generation to generation.
He has shown strength with his arm;

he has scattered the proud in the thoughts of
    their hearts.
He has brought down the powerful from their
    thrones,
and lifted up the lowly;
he has filled the hungry with good things,
and sent the rich away empty.
He has helped his servant Israel,
in remembrance of his mercy,
according to the promise he made to our ancestors,
to Abraham and to his descendants forever.

(Luke 1:46–55; New Revised Standard Version)

❦
Commentaries and Supporting Essays

The Anglican Commentary

Timothy Bradshaw

INTRODUCTION

The background to the Anglican–Roman Catholic International Commission (ARCIC), and all its agreed statements including this latest one concerning Mary, lies in the era of the Second Vatican Council in the 1960s and the Roman Catholic Church's attempt to examine its relationship to the modern cultural context, including other Christian denominations. In 1966 Archbishop Michael Ramsey met Pope Paul VI in Rome and with a view to finding ways of overcoming historic differences they issued a Common Declaration, setting up a dialogue with the aim of producing a unity in truth and faith, the unity for which Jesus prayed. This unity was envisaged to be a "complete communion of faith and sacramental life". From 1970 the Commission, with nine members on each side and representing the two Churches' international spread across the world, met and produced a series of agreed statements. 1971 saw the statement on Eucharistic Doctrine; 1973 that on Ministry and Ordination; 1976 and 1981 on Authority in the Church. The 1988 Lambeth Conference, the international Anglican gathering convened by the Archbishop of Canterbury, resolved that the statements on Eucharist and Ministry were "consonant in substance with the faith of Anglicans", but called for more study on the Authority statement. The Roman Catholic Church responded in 1991 through a text prepared jointly by the Congregation for the Doctrine of the Faith and the Pontifical Council for Promoting Christian Unity, acknowledging some agreement and some remaining differences.

A newly staffed second Commission, ARCIC II, was set up by Pope John Paul II and Archbishop Robert Runcie in 1982. Agreed statements followed entitled *Salvation and the Church* 1987, and *The Church as Communion* 1991, on the nature of the Church. 1994 saw an agreed statement on morals entitled *Life in Christ.* The ongoing question about the authority of the Pope in the Church was taken up again in *The Gift of Authority* 1999. ARCIC had been working primarily on the nature of the Church, its sacraments and ministry, and how authority worked within the Church for its well-being and faithfulness to the message of Jesus. The Church of England's General Synod recently gave some qualified approval to *The Gift of Authority* which argued for accepting the Papacy as an agency for articulating divine will in conjunction with fellow bishops and the whole people of God. There is no doubt that both communions, Roman and Anglican, are serious about restoring unity broken at the time of the Reformation, by a process of self-examination and avoidance of traditional, divisive, ways of stating doctrine.

Ironically the figure of Mary, mother of Jesus and a gentle person in the pages of the New Testament, is another major area of division between the Churches, although Anglicans themselves are used to Anglo-Catholics practising devotions to Mary in churches and by pilgrimages to shrines at places such as Walsingham in the UK. ARCIC II has now issued its agreed statement on this question, as was requested of them in the original Malta Statement in 1968, and again as a result of the meeting of Anglican and Roman Catholic bishops in Mississauga in 2000.

In the earlier ARCIC agreed statement, *Authority in the Church II* (1981), agreement was recorded over Mary as *Theotókos*, God-bearer, and as a model of holiness, a prophetic figure of the Church before and after the incarnation. But major disagreement was registered over the dogmas of the immaculate conception of Mary and her assumption, the teachings that she was conceived in a special way without sin, and that she was taken directly into heaven at the end of her life. Neither of these teachings can be found in the New Testament, and moreover both teachings were made binding on the faithful by decree of the Pope, independently of any church council. These are the key problems to be overcome in this new agreed statement, along with the questions linked to the acceptability of addressing Mary in prayer. ARCIC seeks to remain faithful to the New Testament pattern of faith and worship, using a theology of grace and hope, one rooted also in the experience of Christian worship and devotion. ARCIC invokes the 'Yes and Amen' structure found in the agreed statement *The Gift of Authority* as a means of interpreting Mary's Amen, let it be done to me, in response to the address of the angel. She represents Christian discipleship and obedience.

We will now go through the agreed statement section by section, trying to summarise its teachings, making some comments particularly from an Anglican perspective, and raising some questions.

A MARY ACCORDING TO THE SCRIPTURES

The first section of the statement considers Mary as she appears in the New Testament. This raises the issue of interpreting the texts, and ARCIC is aware that overly 'typological' interpretation can become extravagant, while historical-critical approaches focused on an original meaning can prove 'reductionist'. Typological interpretation gives the Mary found in the biblical narratives the role of an ideal 'type', or perhaps 'icon' in modern secular parlance: she stands for certain truths which can be developed at some length. This way of interpreting the text makes much of the aspect of the meaning of Mary, and this meaning can add further levels of meaning and so become exaggerated. On the other hand, interpreters who focus on the historical side of the narrated Mary, the events that actually happened, may fail to consider her meaning enough, and 'reduce' that meaning to simply what happened. In other words, much depends on how the symbolic meanings attached to the Mary of the New Testament can be taken to extend her historical role into a more transcendent one, and how she could be regarded as having a role in the history of salvation but nothing more. In a sense this, in a nutshell, could be said to be the root of the disagreement between the two Churches.

ARCIC says that it wishes to benefit from the range of modern approaches of interpretation. It begins in the Old Testament, arguing that the witness of Scripture offers a 'trajectory', or perhaps pathway, of grace and hope, of forgiveness and new beginnings. Israel is the covenant partner of God, symbolically his bride and handmaiden. Scripture speaks of a calling of individuals from their first beginnings, for example, Jeremiah, and the 'prevenient', or 'given in advance', grace of God will be a permeating theme of the agreement. Rather like the well-known story of the 'footsteps in the sand', God has been ahead of us to prepare our path. Romans 8:28–30 is cited here as a key text: "those whom God foreknew he predestined to be conformed to the image of his Son … And those whom he called he also justified and those whom he justified he also glorified." This trajectory of grace and hope leads to Christ to fulfil the divine purposes. The role of Israel as the covenant partner of God leads finally to Jesus, by the divine plan of God. As a vital part of this plan, God needs to work through human freedom and consent, and the young Jewish teenage girl Mary gives her full and faithful consent to the divine call to be mother of the Messiah, declaring through her very natural and human puzzlement, "Behold, I am the handmaid of the Lord, let it be to me according to your word" (Luke 1:38). Matthew and Luke refer to Mary specifically in telling the story of Jesus' conception and birth; Mark and John do not, nor does Paul speak of a special mode of Jesus' birth in any way. For Matthew and Luke, descent in the royal line of David emphasises the Messianic expectation, and the virginal conception of Jesus by Mary discloses the radical newness coming with his birth: God is bringing about a completely new phase in his saving activity in human history. In this, ARCIC is in line with the orientation of biblical tradition, so for example we read that Jesus, later in his ministry, as he enters Jerusalem for the last time, rides on a colt "on which no one has ever sat", again symbolising the note of radical newness introduced by Jesus' reign in history. The God of the Bible brings about new and wonderful things in mysterious and surprising ways. Luke's narrative of the annunciation, when the angel

Gabriel comes to Mary and announces her calling (Luke 1:26ff), portrays her, ARCIC says, as uniquely the recipient of election and grace, in line with a series of special births narrated in the Old Testament such as those of Isaac, Samson and Samuel, all children born in the divine plan and by particular divine intervention. Mary's psalm of praise, the *Magnificat* (Luke 1:46ff), stands in this biblical tradition, and ARCIC argues that the *Magnificat* provides the scriptural basis for an appropriate devotion to Mary, since in that psalm she says that all generations will call her "blessed". Mary's agreement to the angel's declaration of her destiny, "let it be to me according to your word", in Latin *fiat*, her Amen to God's will, is given in faith and freedom. Luke also has the premonition of pain for Mary later, (Luke 2:34) "a sword will pierce your soul", pointing ahead to suffering involved in her vocation and ministry as the mother of Jesus.

In the Gospels of Matthew and Luke, Jesus is conceived by the Holy Spirit, miraculously, without the biological fatherhood of Joseph, Mary's betrothed, who nevertheless sticks by Mary, taking her at her word. Mary thus conceives the baby without losing her virginity. Matthew narrates this by saying, "before they came together she was found to be with child of the Holy Spirit" (Matthew 1:18). ARCIC teaches that this "virginal conception" (§18) is primarily a sign of divine presence, the work of the Spirit, rather perhaps than a description as might be given in a biological textbook. Footnote 2 rejects any notion that the virginal conception is analogous to a magical coming together of supernature and nature, as if some pagan mythical story. ARCIC wishes to stress the meaning of the story, and indeed sets it together with the "new birth of every Christian" by water and the Spirit (John 3:3–5), avoiding the sense of Jesus' conception and birth as "an isolated miracle" (§18). ARCIC in footnote 3 of their statement notes that the New Testament speaks of Jesus' brothers, with the implication that Mary had other children following Jesus' birth. But ARCIC suggests that they may refer to kinsmen or relatives rather than literal brothers.

Having discussed the conception and birth of Jesus, ARCIC (§19) moves on to "Mary and the True Family of Jesus", taking its cue from the incident in Mark's Gospel where Jesus' mother and brothers come and wait for Jesus, wanting to speak to him (Mark 3:31). There Jesus distances himself from his 'natural' family, stressing instead those who do the will of God, the family of faith or his 'eschatological family', his new family rooted in the Kingdom of God rather than blood relationships. His natural mother Mary seems at first to lack deep understanding of his mission, but this is said to develop as for other disciples. In Acts 1:14 Mary and Jesus' brothers are depicted as waiting with the apostles for the coming of the Pentecostal Spirit, the birth of the Church.

Mary in John's Gospel (§23) is interpreted as herself entering into discipleship and faith, as compared with only a blood relationship, at the feast at Cana (John 2:8). There Jesus asks Mary "O woman, what have you to do with me?", when Mary tells him that there is no wine. ARCIC suggests that the natural bonds between mother and son give way to the new relationship rooted in faith in God and his kingdom coming in Jesus. Mary becomes a disciple with a role of helping others come to Jesus (§25). John's Gospel notes Jesus' words from the cross to his disciples, "behold your mother", indicating not only a real care for her but also a wider motherly role for Mary in the Church, according to ARCIC (§26). Jesus addresses Mary directly from the cross as "woman", and ARCIC expands this with a Mary-Eve typology (§27), affirming that Mary is on a spiritual level "mother of all who gain true life from the water and blood that flow from the side of Christ". This is a "symbolic and corporate reading" (§27). In this light, says ARCIC, it is difficult to speak of the Church without thinking of Mary as its first realization.

The book of Revelation and its reference to the "woman" is taken as meaning the people of God, the Church, oppressed by Satan. But some patristic writers came to think of Mary when reading this narrative.

Overall, the scriptural witness summons all believers to call Mary blessed as the handmaid of the Lord, who suffered for her faithfulness. ARCIC wishes to weave us, the present readers of Scripture, into the narratives about Mary and the apostles, for example, that we are at one with them as they pray for the outpouring of the Spirit on the Church. We may even glimpse in her the final destiny of God's people to conquer sin and death (§30).

Questions many Anglicans will be asking of ARCIC's treatment of the Scripture passages on Mary will include that of the brothers of Jesus, and why the plain meaning of these references should be altered, indeed whether such alteration is justified as fair interpretation and whether Jesus having brothers should be problematic. The style of ARCIC's interpretation is often to take up symbolic meanings of a

narrative and develop these, for example the movement from Mary as 'woman' to her as a second Eve.
The suggestion that Mary moves from the role of
natural mother to that of disciple in the new family,
or perhaps kingdom, of Jesus, is an interesting one.
Mary is described by ARCIC so far as the humble
young Jewish woman who freely agrees to take up
the vocation given her, and whose relationship to
her son develops into that of disciple. There is no
doubt that this section on Scripture will provide
much common ground.

Possible questions to consider

Have Anglicans generally failed to give proper attention
to Mary in Scripture, and if so, why?

Why is the possibility of Jesus having brothers a sensitive one for ARCIC, and is it faced honestly?

How might it be helpful to think of Mary as a member
of Jesus' natural family, and also, later, as a disciple in
his eschatological family of faith?

What do you think of the way ARCIC interprets the
relevant texts historically and symbolically?

Do you agree that Mary should be regarded as the New
Eve, paralleling Jesus as the New Adam?

Does the role of the Holy Spirit in the narratives of
Mary and Jesus receive sufficient attention?

B Mary in the Christian Tradition

The statement moves on to reflect on the history of discussion of Mary in the Church. The early paragraphs in this section, (§31ff), deal with the Christological controversies, the debates attempting best to shape a Christian definition of Jesus as both fully human and fully divine. Part of these debates was the Greek word *Theotókos*, 'God-bearer' or 'Mother of God', as a proper title for Mary. This word became part of the historic Chalcedonian Definition agreed in 451 at Chalcedon, a city near the Black Sea. Why was this word so important? It was regarded as confirming a crystal-clear statement about the very identity of Jesus, who he actually was and is, his very self or 'person'. The theologians and bishops came to the conclusion that they could not do justice to this question by describing Jesus only as an inspired man, indwelt by the Spirit or the Word, as found for example in the case of Jeremiah, to whom the word of the Lord said "Before I formed you in the womb I knew you, and before you were born I consecrated you; I appointed you a prophet to the nations" (Jeremiah 1:5). At Chalcedon it was decided to recognise that Jesus was the Word or Son of God, of the same being as God the Father. That is his identity, and this Trinitarian Son has assumed a full human nature. Mary therefore gave birth to none other than this divine Son of God, he was the baby born to her, humanly. The title *Theotókos* for Mary safeguards the humanity of Jesus and his identity as the divine Word. Mary gave birth to her son of her own substance, he did not just appear to be human; he did not descend from heaven in a heavenly body, nor when he was born did he simply pass through his mother. The Chalcedonian Definition specifically enshrined the term *Theotókos* of Mary (§34). The councils of Nicea and Chalcedon have always been authoritative for Anglicans in upholding the divine person of Christ with his full human nature, and the title of *Theotókos* accordingly as fitting for Mary. So far therefore there is full accord between the Roman Catholic and Anglican doctrines of Mary and Jesus, both stand in the 'Ancient Common Tradition'.

ARCIC now takes us on to the issue of "The Celebration of Mary in the Ancient Common Traditions" (§35), charting the growth of piety in relation to Mary in heaven. This begins with the theological significance of the "cloud of witnesses" (Hebrews 12:1) and the communion of saints gone before. Mary came to have a special place in this heavenly communion and scriptural themes were adapted accordingly, notably

those of Mary as the New Eve and as the quintes-
sential figure representing the ideal Church as obedient and faithful. Reflection on the place of Mary
in the communion of saints and her motherly care
prompted devotion as a deeply sympathetic figure
and prayer, both private and public. Some early
Christian theologians linked the theme of Jesus as
second Adam reversing the disobedience of the first
Adam to that of Mary as the second Eve overcoming sin and providing a new Eve for the human race,
linked to Jesus. Her historical role as his mother has
developed, through a consideration of the communion of saints in heaven, into a role as second Eve in
solidarity with the human race, as is the second
Adam. Some early Christian theologians link the
theme of Jesus as the second Adam, reversing the
disobedience of the first Adam, with that of Mary as
the second Eve, since she was obedient to God in
contrast to the first Eve on behalf of the human race,
in a way parallel to her Son's obedience.

ARCIC points out that in Christian history Mary's
obedience shown in history is translated to a heavenly role, and she becomes a model of holiness. This
is associated with her virginal conception of Jesus,
and she gradually gained the title 'Ever Virgin'. In a
long footnote ARCIC explains that this title

involves Mary not only being a virgin at the conception of Jesus, but that "As Austrine wrote, 'she conceived him as a virgin, she gave birth as a virgin, she remained a virgin'". Clearly this claim stretches the New Testament evidence, and is linked to the references to the brothers of Jesus and the argument that these were not in fact brothers but other kinsmen. The idea of the perpetual virginity of Mary was at the same time taken to symbolise her inner attitudes of openness to God, obedience and faith, the model of Christian discipleship. This then extended to the idea that Mary was sinless, as Augustine is quoted as teaching. The title 'all-holy' can be found in church life by the sixth century. Devotion to her flourished following the Chalcedonian title *Theotókos*, with texts and images celebrating her holiness, praying with her, praising her and asking her protection (§39). Celebration of Mary was written into liturgies. Feasts developed concerning the end and beginning of her life, her conception being celebrated in England in the early eleventh century (§40). Legendary stories influenced the growth of the idea that she was taken into heaven, or 'assumed', in a special way at the end of her life, without suffering death. She became part of the victorious Church triumphant in heaven, the glorified body of Jesus, the Church.

ARCIC goes on to consider "The growth of Marian Doctrine and Devotion in the Middle Ages", including some criticism of some of these developments (§41). During this era the humanity of Jesus was dwelt upon by theologians and, in parallel, so were the virtues and merits of Mary. Christ and Mary became linked in devotional life, and practices such as the rosary developed. Christian art reflected this rich mixture of spirituality. Mary's role as an ideal type of the Church grew. But ARCIC tells us that she gradually was placed in a mediatorial position, dispensing the graces of Christ *to* the Church. Mary's sinlessness was affirmed, to the point where she was considered possibly to have been 'immaculate' from the day of her conception. She came to occupy a role as worker of miracles and intermediary between God and humanity, in what ARCIC calls "the florid Marian devotion of the Late Middle Ages" (§43).

The Reformation is then described in relation to this spirituality. It pruned back the florid growth and abuses, attempting to regain the central focus on Christ's salvation but, according to ARCIC, may have overdone the pruning in their desire to ensure the centrality of Christ as sole mediator. ARCIC speaks of the Reformation as a radical 're-reception' of Scripture and the doctrine of Jesus as the sole mediator. The Reformers continued to honour Mary, but in her role as historical partner in the saving story of Jesus. Latimer and Cranmer followed the tradition they had inherited by accepting Mary as 'ever virgin' (§45). The Reformers did not affirm or deny Mary's sinlessness, but they strongly stress the universality of sin and the need for Christ's redemption. The Book of Common Prayer omitted the feast of Mary's Assumption, as lacking scriptural warrant. Nevertheless Mary's great psalm of praise, the *Magnificat*, is part and parcel of the Anglican service of Evening Prayer.

The Counter Reformation ensured that Mary was a distinguishing marker against Protestantism. Her devotion flourished in the nineteenth century, so that popular devotional pressure built up leading to the Pope defining the dogma of the Immaculate Conception of Mary in 1854, a dogma necessary for all Roman Catholic faithful to accept as infallibly true. 1950 similarly saw the declaration of the dogma of Mary's Assumption into heaven. In the twentieth century, in 1964, Vatican II is thought by some commentators to have under-emphasized devotions to Mary, and Pope Paul VI had to foster such devotions again, but within the doctrines of Christ and the

Church. He commended the saying of the Angelus and the Rosary as within these criteria, as did Pope John Paul II. It has to be noted here that ARCIC does not discuss the very great stress placed on Mary by Pope John Paul II as the guide through his life, nor the excommunication of Fr Tissa Balasuriya for his book on Mary, *Mary and Human Liberation* 1997, on the grounds that it played down her freedom from the taint of original sin.

Anglicans (§49) are said to have given Mary a new prominence in worship through liturgies, and a 're-reception' of the place of Mary is claimed to have taken place within both Churches. She is seen by both communions as the New Eve and a type of the Church (§51). ARCIC stresses the place of Mary with the saints in their ongoing prayer for the Church in history. Mary is inseparably linked to Christ and the Church.

POSSIBLE QUESTIONS TO CONSIDER

Does the title 'God-bearer' or *Theotókos*, agreed by all Churches as appropriate, help you understand who Jesus is?

What do you make of the idea that Mary was and is 'Ever Virgin', even after the birth of Jesus? Does this help or hinder our understanding of the incarnation?

Have we appreciated fully the fact that the humanity of Jesus is of Mary?

Assess ARCIC's presentation of the claim that Mary was wholly sinless.

From the praiseworthy motive of paying due honour to Mary in wholeheartedly obeying the divine calling, how and why did the cult of Mary get out of control in the High Middle Ages? How should the Church prevent Mary obscuring Christ as sympathetic mediator with us?

Do you agree with ARCIC that the correct attitude to Mary is a reformed Roman Catholic one, guarded with a strong doctrine of Christ?

Is the idea of being part of the communion of saints, earthly and heavenly, a new one for you, and is there warrant for being in conscious communion with individual saints in glory?

C MARY WITHIN THE PATTERN OF GRACE AND HOPE

This section (§52-63) seeks to provide the theological rationale for overcoming the major disagreements set out by ARCIC I, stated above. The method is that of reading back from fulfilment to inception, a kind of retroactive principle. We are bidden to view the economy of grace from its fulfilment in Christ back into history (§52). Romans 8:30 is cited here, appealing to divine predestinating action, working out in historical life. Mary is to be called blessed in the future at her calling by Gabriel; she embodies the elect Israel of whom Paul speaks in Romans 8:30. God was at work in Mary from the start of her life. We have no history of the end of her life, but some analogies from Scripture indicate that she might have entered glory without tasting death (§56); this is part of the pattern of anticipated eschatology. She is a sign of hope for all humanity. She is a new creation, the type of the Church, and a disciple.

The papal definitions can now be explained in terms of divine purpose (§58). The dogma of the Assumption is rendered plausible by way of stretching the logic of hope and glory, indeed as a dogma it defines a fact of history, otherwise unknowable. The issue of Mary's Immaculate Conception, defined in 1854, is considered by way of her Son's redeeming work being retrospectively implied to her from the conception of her life, so avoiding the problem of her not needing his redemption because of an inherent sinlessness (§59). She is preserved from the stain of original sin by God's constant mercy in the economy of grace by divine predestination.

ARCIC's presentation of Mary full of grace, predestined for her role in the divine plan of salvation, is strikingly reminiscent of a very similar treatment of Christ proposed by the Scottish theologian Donald Baillie, albeit a Christology which has been found by critics to offer a picture of inspiration rather than of full incarnation. Baillie suggested the best way of understanding Christ was by way of the analogy of grace and its paradoxical nature as we experience it. We are free and yet as disciples can look back and see divine grace has in fact been sustaining us despite our feelings of desperation and weakness. The paradox is that we act freely, and yet God's grace is at work in and through our free choices. Likewise the paradox of sin and grace is that when we sin we blame ourselves, but when we do what is right the Christian disciple gives the glory to God. Jesus lived out this paradox of grace to the fullest extent, being wholly open to divine grace and wholly human. Baillie says that we can trace this prevenient grace back to the intention of God. God was in Christ by the grace of God. His battle with sin was won in this way, through full human freedom constantly exercised according to God's will.

ARCIC similarly argues of Mary that God was at work in her by grace from her earliest beginnings, and the paradox is that she was fully and freely obedient to the divine will. In that way she can be said to be sinless, rather than by way of special and different sort of conception or inherent sinlessness by nature. The end of Mary's life on earth, ARCIC says, is not directly revealed in Scripture or historical evidence. However, by analogy with figures such as Elijah who was taken up into heaven in a whirlwind, and the penitent thief on the cross with Jesus who is promised an immediate place with Jesus in paradise, ARCIC reflects that the idea of Mary being assumed into heaven by God gains some plausibility. ARCIC argues that the spiritual merit and destiny of Mary could appropriately be consummated by such an assumption into heaven. This Old Testament analogy is taken to be an anticipation of the destiny of all disciples, the Church, and also a sign of hope for all humanity. If we asked ARCIC whether Mary's assumption into heaven as a sign of hope to humanity might be in danger of displacing, or obscuring the place of Christ's resurrection as the truest sign of that hope, ARCIC might respond that Mary's assumption shares in the messianic destiny of Jesus, or that she follows in his pathway which he has pioneered. This kind of argumentation will inevitably provide much food for thought, particularly on the part of Anglicans who are being invited to accept this logic of deriving historical events from spiritual symbolism about Mary in the economy of grace.

The Anglican problem that the papal dogmatic definitions, for Roman Catholics, are in effect revealed by God (§60) by virtue of their status, is discussed in the light of changing contexts and understandings of revelation. The dogmas are presented by ARCIC as a kind of witness to revelation, perhaps akin to the rabbinical 'fence around the law'. When such truths expressed in the papal dogmas are affirmed as revealed by God, "there is no suggestion of new revelation". ARCIC's earlier *Gift of Authority* developed a method of showing such claims to be in conformity with Scripture by not conflicting with it (§61). The papal dogmas gave voice to the consensus of faith among believers in communion with the Bishop of Rome, and were reaffirmed by Vatican II. Anglicans are said to need, at the very least, the consent of an ecumenical council for such teaching to become *de fide*, a concept itself raising some major questions for Anglicans, lay and ordained (§62). Most Anglicans would need strong scriptural warrant for such doctrinal obligation as the basis for an ecumenical council's decision. ARCIC notes that these definitions are not open to disagreement if full communion is restored between the two Churches: "Roman Catholics find it hard to envisage a restoration of communion in which acceptance of certain doctrines would be requisite for some and not for others" (§63). But then, on the other hand, the importance of these dogmas should not be exaggerated and should be viewed in the light of the agreed *Theotókos* doctrine. The doctrinal presentation of the dogmas in this predestinarian, eschatological way is thought to be a means of gaining common agreement in a mutual 're-reception' involving a regrounding of the dogmas as seen in new, less harsh, light. The doctrine of the sinlessness of Mary is rooted in divine grace, for example, rather than in a miraculously sinless nature different to ours. ARCIC argues that this reinterpretation of the papal dogmas would then clear the path for acceptance of Roman Catholic Marian doctrine and devotion, to which ARCIC now returns.

POSSIBLE QUESTIONS TO CONSIDER

Does the perfected, ideal, obedient human discipleship of Mary depicted in ARCIC possibly obscure the significance to Christians of the humanity of Jesus, in which we share by baptism and faith?

How might the role of Mary as the type and representative of the Church be accommodated to that of
Christ as 'head of the body', and as the bridegroom
of the bride?

Is there a danger of equating sex with sinful behaviour
in some of the language about the purity of Mary in
her role of 'ever virgin', and does this do justice to
the Christian view of creation?

Do you find the way ARCIC presents Mary and the
Roman Catholic doctrines about her, in the light of
divine calling and hope, offers a possible way to
overcome existing disagreements about her role?

D MARY IN THE LIFE OF THE CHURCH

Mary's 'Amen' to God's 'Yes' in Christ includes her role
in the historical and in the eschatological family of
Jesus. Anglicans have focused on her ministry in the
example given in Scripture of her obedience and
discipleship. Roman Catholics, expanding on this,
have "given prominence to the ongoing ministry of
Mary in the economy of grace and the communion
of saints. Mary points people to Christ, commending them to him and helping them to share his life"
(§65). For most Anglicans, the role of the Holy
Spirit is expressed in precisely these terms; a point
not considered by ARCIC. Mary is agreed to be the

fullest example of the life of grace, she is alive in Christ and we should walk together with her, Christ's foremost disciple.

Mary has a special place in the history of salvation and so in liturgical and private prayer, prayers are said with her, as with the saints, constantly praying before God. This brings ARCIC to the issue of intercession and mediation in the communion of saints, a practice known to the Anglo-Catholic wing of Anglicanism, but hardly in general. The practice of asking Mary to intercede grew after the declaration of her being declared *Theotókos*. The prayer "Hail Mary" had the final phrase added in the fifteenth Century, "pray for us sinners, now and at the hour of our death", and is often taken by evangelicals to indicate a lack of confidence in the finished work of Christ as sufficient for salvation. Reformers rejected the invocation of the saints as obscuring the clarity of the mediation of Christ and the Spirit; Article XXII asserting the idea has no warrant in Scripture. The Roman Catholic Council of Trent and Vatican II on the other hand teach that such prayer is harmless and indeed helpful if made through Christ. The role of Mary as maternal towards the whole human race becomes the way this is commended by ARCIC, not obscuring or diminishing the unique mediation of Christ (§67). The Roman Catholic position is presented now as the moderate centre ground, neither exaggerating nor minimising Mary's role. Obviously the need for such a maternal mediation, and the question of whether it does not inevitably make Mary the sympathetic figure who can and will pass on our all too human requests to the now rather severe Christ, arises in the Anglican reader's mind.

ARCIC argues that all ministries of the Church use human means, but that this mediation does not lessen that of Christ. The prayer of the Church stands in Christ, not as a parallel prayer, and is enabled by the Holy Spirit. Asking friends to pray for us does not conflict with Christ's work, but is a "means whereby this can be displayed" (§68). Stretching this point further, we pray in the company of the faithful both here and departed, and for some this intuition of the presence of departed friends deepens a sense of being in Christ across time and in solidarity with the saints, especially with Mary (§69). We are bidden in Scripture to ask others to pray for us, and we can again stretch this to the faithful departed in the body of Christ; requests for assistance in prayer can be made to holy members of the communion of saints (§70). This notion is not directly found in Scripture, but on the other

hand is not unscriptural, argues ARCIC, not dis-
cussing the Old Testament tradition against making
contact with the dead. ARCIC teaches that no practice must obscure the trinitarian economy of grace.
"The Distinctive Ministry of Mary" (§71) is that of
assisting others through her active prayer; many
experience empathy and solidarity with her especially when her historical life parallels theirs. This
ministry again seems to echo that of the Paraclete
and Holy Spirit. In suffering she represents a figure
of tenderness and compassion. She is also the
mother of humanity, the new Eve. We may come to
see her as such (§72), although it must be said
equally that many do not. Many (§73) find this
devotion enriches their worship of God and local
customs should be respected, including apparitions
of Mary, which become focal points of spiritual
comfort, and of course were greatly encouraged by
Pope John Paul II. This kind of cult is classified as
private devotion, and is deemed to be not required
(§73) of the faithful, merely permitted and respected
—a classification which most Anglicans would
request for a good deal of what ARCIC commends.
The liberationist note found in the *Magnificat* finds a
place (§74), that is to say the orientation of Mary's
historical life and commitment can arguably chime

in with the Christian imperative to focus especially on the plight of the poor, displaced and hopeless. In conclusion ARCIC thinks no reason now exists for disagreement on this matter, given its theological re-reception argued above.

ARCIC has sought to explain what Roman Catholics believe about Mary and why they offer prayer and devotion to her in heaven, and expect her to provide protection and sympathetic care, indeed to offer her presence to Christians across time and space, as Pope John Paul II very obviously did. ARCIC explains that Roman Catholics would not find it difficult to accept Anglicans into full communion if they could not agree to the full scope of Roman Catholic Marian piety, preferring instead a kind of 'live and let live' approach to which they are used on such matters in their own communion. ARCIC has certainly striven to show that Scripture has a range of material on Mary, and that it can be read as containing symbolism which in turn can be used to justify Roman Catholic belief and practice. It might be worth pointing out that another Anglican agreed statement, for some reason rather neglected, could be said to have reached a similar conclusion. The Anglican — Orthodox Dublin Agreed Statement 1984 contains this paragraph:

All prayer is ultimately addressed to the Trinitarian God. We pray to God the Father through our Lord Jesus Christ in the Holy Spirit. The Church is united in a single movement of worship with the Church in heaven, with the Blessed Virgin Mary, 'with angels and archangels and all the company of heaven'. The Orthodox also pray to the Blessed Virgin Mary and Theotokos and the saints as friends and living images of Christ (p.34, §66).

There is no doubt that much hangs on this view of the Church spanning earth and heaven, our communion with those who have gone before, and the legitimacy of contacting these heavenly disciples in glory for help and comfort here and now.

POSSIBLE QUESTIONS TO CONSIDER

Should ARCIC have included some reference to the feminist cultural and theological movements in relation to Mary and 're-reception' of Marian dogmas?

Is the role of Mary as sympathetic maternal figure in heaven a help to feminist Christians? Do Anglicans miss the comforts offered by this glorified maternal figure?

Is ARCIC open to theological criticism in rarely speaking of the ministry of the Holy Spirit and

explaining that in relation to the similar role presented for Mary now in helping disciples?

Should ARCIC have discussed actual incidences of
Marian piety, together with their social and political
contexts, such as those of Lourdes, Fatima, and
Medjugorje, especially in the light of their importance to Pope John Paul II?

Should Anglicans be allowed to respect Marian dogmas
symbolically while not accepting them literally?

CONCLUSION

ARCIC offers this proposal as a means whereby Anglicans
can try to understand or get inside Roman Catholic
doctrines, dogmas and piety concerning Mary. For
some Anglicans of the more Catholic persuasion this
will already seem very familiar and congenial. For
others, probably the majority, it will seem strange, particularly the last two sections as they expand upon the
New Testament and patristic theological doctrines.

Evangelicals will be greatly interested in the initial scriptural section, as well as committed to the *Theotókos* title
for Mary, institutionalised by Chalcedon. They may
find it hard to relate to the expansion of Mary as
earthly mother of Jesus into Mary as 'metaphysical' or
heavenly maternal figure for all the world, and in touch
with disciples across time and space. And Evangelicals

retain the concern to focus on Christ as the great high priest whose humanity has passed into the heavens on our behalf, our new Adam, our new 'covenant head'. Mary's role as the ideal type or representative of the Church seems to shadow this Christological ministry and this will stimulate important discussion.

Liberal Anglicans will often be happy to theologise in terms of the symbolic meaning of narratives and the experience of the Church today. They will no doubt be concerned about possible obligatory status for Marian doctrines or dogmas for which the evidence is primarily that of spirituality. The issue of authority will be of interest to all Anglicans, especially since they are used to living in a pluralistic kind of Church content to embrace friendly disagreement on secondary matters. There is no doubt that ARCIC has been honest in producing a document in basically a Roman Catholic mode so that Anglicans can get the feel of what is being needed by Roman Catholics in any reunited Church.

Mary herself, whatever her present role in heaven, must be saddened to know she is a focus of disagreement, and has been used as a badge of division between Christians. She surely will be rejoicing that efforts are being made to remedy this.

The Roman Catholic Commentary

Jared Wicks, S.J.

In Chapter III of *Ut unum sint*, Pope John Paul II named five doctrinal topics which need fuller study to promote movement on the way from the present basic doctrinal unity toward a true consensus in faith between the Catholic Church and her partners in ecumenical dialogue. Among areas needing examination, one is "the Virgin Mary, as Mother of God and Icon of the Church, the spiritual Mother who intercedes for Christ's disciples and for all humanity" (UUS 79). Here, on the Virgin Mary, Catholic convictions of faith and devotional practice seem to have little resonance in the churches and communities whose faith and life was shaped by Reformation.

The importance of Mary in the quest for full communion was further underscored in Summer 2000, when the special consultation of Anglican and Catholic bishops, held at Mississauga, Canada, requested that the Anglican-Roman Catholic International Commission (ARCIC) turn its attention of the place of Mary in the life and doctrine of the Church.

To this request the Commission has responded admirably in the present document, *Mary: Grace and Hope in Christ*, which offers to the churches a lucid proposal (1) that in faith convictions about Mary, Anglicans and Catholics are in substantial agreement, while (2) their differences over prayers which invoke Mary's aid are not ecclesially divisive.

STARTING POINT

One reason for the success of this latest phase of dialogue is that it did not begin from zero in examining Anglican and Catholic convictions concerning Mary. The 1981 Windsor Statement of ARCIC, *Authority in the Church II*, while registering Anglican difficulties over the biblical basis of the Marian dogmas of 1854 and 1950, could still sketch a foundational starting point for further study:

Anglicans and Roman Catholics can agree in much of the truth that these two dogmas are designed to

affirm. We agree that there can be but one mediator between God and man, Jesus Christ, and reject
any interpretation of the role of Mary which
obscures this affirmation. We agree in recognizing
that Christian understanding of Mary is inseparably
linked with the doctrines of Christ and the Church.
We agree in recognizing the grace and unique
vocation of Mary, Mother of God Incarnate
(*Theotókos*), in observing her festivals, and in
according her honour in the communion of
saints. We agree that she was prepared by divine
grace to be the mother of the Redeemer, by whom
she herself was redeemed and received into
glory. We further agree in recognizing in Mary
a model of holiness, obedience and faith for all
Christians. We accept that it is possible to regard
her as a prophetic figure of the Church of God
before as well as after the Incarnation (*Authority II*,
no. 30).

The present statement, *Mary: Grace and Hope in Christ*,
after citing the passage just given (§2, also in §76),
revisits this cluster of shared convictions and extends
them, by first developing a solid biblical theology
of Mary (Part A) and then reviewing the history
of Marian faith and practice, both in the common

history and during the centuries of Anglican-Catholic divisions (Part B). Part C offers a creative theological analysis of Marian doctrine from the surprisingly fruitful perspective of the eschatological teleology   of God's work of grace and salvation, before Part   D examines the respective practice of prayer and devotion to Mary among Anglicans and Catholics.[1]

This commentary will begin by examining selected insights formulated in the four parts of the statement, before a second section looks more in detail at two points of particular interest, namely, the biblical methodology of Part A and the eschatological perspective of Part C. A third section will offer two further considerations stimulated by *Mary: Grace and Hope in Christ* which may help other ecumenical exchanges on Mary.

---

1 When ARCIC began its new study of Mary, it could also look to two recent dialogue-documents, (1) *The One Mediator, the Saints, and Mary*, from the 8th round of the Lutheran-Catholic dialogue in the US (Minneapolis: Augsburg Press 1992), and (2) *Marie dans le dessein de Dieu and la communion des saints*, by the Groupe des Dombes (Paris: Bayard /Centurion 1999), translated as *Maria nel disegno di Dio e nella comunione dei santi* (Magnano: Qigajon 1998) and *Mary in the Plan of God and the Communion of Saints* (New York: Paulist 2002). I reviewed these contributions in "The Virgin Mary in Recent Ecumenical Dialogues", *Gregorianum* 81 (2000), 25–75.

I. MARY IN SCRIPTURE, HISTORY, THEOLOGY, AND DEVOTIONAL PRACTICE

An important methodological point, stated in §3, concerns the ongoing reception of the Tradition of Christian faith and life delivered once and for all by the Apostles. Here ARCIC draws on its previous text, *The Gift of Authority* (1999), to highlight the paradoxical combination of continuity and renewal in such reception, for in any given age the Church and its members lay hold of the meaning of the apostolic heritage in ways that fall short of a full vision of salvation in Christ. We see through a glass clouded by our historical limitations. But ongoing biblical study, especially when linked with the basic structures of worship and promoted by fresh spiritual insight ("the wisdom of holy persons"), can bring the church both to new understandings of the meaning of God's saving word and work as well as to corrections of previously held imperfect understandings.[2]

---

2 *The Gift of Authority*, nos. 24-25. The fact – and fruitfulness – of ongoing reception was stated by Vatican II, both in its doctrine of positive developments in grasping the meaning of apostolic tradition ("There is growth in insight into the realities and words that are being passed on. … Thus … the church is always advancing toward the plenitude of divine truth." DV 8,2) and in the Council's counterbalancing admission that concerning life, discipline, and the formulation of doctrine, "Christ summons the church, as she goes her pilgrim way, to that continual reformation of which she always has need, insofar as she is a human institution on earth" (UR 6).

As we live in unfolding history, there are thus events of re-reception of transmitted doctrines and components of Christian practice. Today, in the setting of our ecumenical commitment, renewed reception takes place along with our ecumenical partners, as we probe together the Christian sources to lay hold afresh of the significance of events and persons in the economy of salvation—specifically here of Mary's role in this work of God's grace through Christ—in ways that promote greater communion in faith and reconciliation of church practices.

MARY IN SCRIPTURE

ARCIC's new text sets the stage for its biblical reconsideration of Mary by positing in §8-10 the theme of God's covenant with Israel, which stands in service of an intended blessing for all the families of the earth (Genesis 12:3, 26:4, 28:14; Sirach 44:22). But within this universal vision, the Scriptures of Israel prepare more directly the consideration of Mary by telling of individuals granted God's calling and enabling grace for particular roles in the unfolding of God's purposes (§10). The coherent line of preparation leading to Jesus' messianic and universal saving action includes as well the roles of Sarah and Hannah, "whose sons fulfilled the purposes of God for his people" (§11).

In the Gospels, Matthew 1–2, treated in §12–13, sketches a movement from Abraham and the fulfillment of Israel's messianic expectation to the coming of the Magi from beyond the borders of Israel to do homage to the child whom they find with Mary his mother. The opening narrative of Jesus' virginal conception, birth, and revelation elegantly anticipates the overall movement of the First Gospel from Jesus' teaching in Galilee and Jerusalem to the confession of Jesus as Son of God by the Roman centurion (Matthew 27:54) and to the Risen Lord's mandate to the eleven to make disciples of all nations (28:20).

In Luke 1–2, §14–17 notes how Mary's *Magnificat* anticipates the reversal that is central to Jesus' message of God's reign and how her spirituality of thoughtful pondering of words and events (Luke 2:19.51), coupled with suffering (2:48-50), shows individuals and communities the true inwardness of faith. The annunciation by Gabriel is replete with echoes of previous events and formulations, like the "overshadowing" power of God, which echoes both the brooding Spirit of Genesis 1:2 and God's presence covering the Ark and Tabernacle (Exodus 25:20, 40:35). The Third Gospel sets clearly the outer framework of action by Father, Son, and Holy

Spirit, within which Mary declares her *fiat* to God's work, animated by God's favour that enveloped her life.

The birth narratives of two Gospels give independent witness to Jesus' virginal conception by the Holy Spirit, on which §18 cautions us not to see an empty space of absence, but instead a pointer to the work of the Spirit, who takes initiatives and carries God's saving project through to completion in responsive human beings.

§21 cites a little-noticed Lukan contribution to relating Mary and the church in Acts 1:14, where the eleven await the empowering promise of the Father in constant prayer with Mary and the other women. (From this, medieval Western iconography could give Mary a place in the community of Pentecost, under the tongues of fire, at times with the open Scriptures before her.)

On the Fourth Gospel, where Mary appears at Cana and at the cross of her son, the new document moves to levels beyond a simple narrative reading, that is, to meanings for which the narrative of events is said to leave room (§24). To this we will return in Section 2, below.

At Cana, Mary's pointed observation, "They have no wine", expresses Israel's longing for the feast of the messianic kingdom, while her imperative "Do whatever he tells you", comes from a believer now within the messianic community. Beyond the surface of Jesus' words from the cross to his mother and the beloved disciple, the text of John 19:25–7 gives Mary a maternal role in the church, since the Fourth Gospel presents this disciple as the beginning of the church, that is, as object of Jesus' love, faithful follower, and reliable witness (§26).

To complete its biblical study, MGH notes that the "woman" of Revelation 12 seems to be primarily a representative figure of God's people under the onslaught of persecution, but still her giving birth to a child destined to rule has led some to find the text illuminating Mary's association with her son in his eschatological victory (§29).

MARIAN DOCTRINE AND DEVOTION IN HISTORY

Receiving early dogmatic developments, Anglicans and Catholics are agreed in holding to Jesus being truly born of Mary, to Mary reversing the fateful legacy of the disobedient 'virgin Eve' by conceiving of the Holy Spirit, and to the validity of protecting the oneness of Christ's person by affirming Mary to be the God-bearer, *Theotókos*. Augustine is cited approvingly on God's gift to Mary of an "abundance of grace for overcoming sin in every particular", which other Fathers see as given from Mary's origin to prepare her for a unique vocation as Mother of the Lord (§38).

By the sixth century Mary was singled out in most Eucharistic prayers as first among the saints, in communion with whom the church praises the Father in the memorial of Christ's saving deed. The popular prayer for Mary's protection, *Sub tuum praesidium*,[3] comes from the fifth century, from the time after the Council of Ephesus when churches, like St Mary Major, were being dedicated to Mary and days of the year were being marked out as her feasts (§39–40).

Medieval devotion to the humanity of Jesus the Saviour (Bernard, Francis of Assisi), shown forth in statuary and stained glass, led believers to also attend lovingly to his mother. In the universities, questions about the causality of the redemption effected by Christ also led to pondering the role played by Mary and her role then in applying her Son's saving graces to needy humans. While St Thomas was measured in treating Mary's sanctification, Duns Scotus applied the general notion of prevenient operative grace to conclude to Mary being without sin from the first

3 The text is given in MGH 39, note 9.

moment of her conception. Many believers, during late medieval trials, had recourse to Mary's protection, individually and in confraternities, in ways that left little room for her glorified son's high-priestly mediation (§41–3).

While the English Reformation brought a purification of devotional life, it held to Mary as *Theotókos* and ever-Virgin, with only Mary's Assumption being suppressed as wanting in biblical warrant (§44–6).

When Tridentine Catholicism insisted on Marian doctrine and devotion as an identifying characteristic, it had the effect, among others, of solidifying the presence in the lived faith of Catholics of convictions about her Immaculate Conception and Assumption, as was ascertained before the dogmatic definitions of 1854 and 1950. Vatican II brought a paradigmatic re-reception of biblical and patristic Marian themes, exemplified by the choice to make the independently prepared schema *De beata Virgine* into Ch. VIII of the Constitution on the Church, *Lumen Gentium*, which thus moves from Christ the light of the nations through eight ample chapters of ecclesiology to conclude with an expression in LG 69 of the ecumenical hope that Mary, a sign of hope and comfort, will by her intercession before her Son hasten the gathering of all people into the one people of God (§47).

With the recent move among Anglicans to mention Mary in eucharistic prayers and to celebrate on 15 August a principal Marian feast (§50), the new document finds a central agreement in our two communions in honouring Mary and believing that she prays for the whole Church, with which she is inseparably linked. On this basis a fresh approach can be made to the Catholic Marian dogmas (§49–51).

THEOLOGICAL INSIGHTS INTO MARIAN DOGMAS

Mary: Grace and Hope in Christ establishes a new biblical framework in §52–3 for its theological consideration of Mary's distinctive place in the economy of God's grace, especially the place of one conceived without sin and assumed into heaven. The luminous framework is that of a largely Pauline doctrine of our graced call and destiny, by which our final sharing in Christ's glory has already begun. We will return to this eschatological perspective in Section 2, below.

Scripture knows of God caring for his servants before birth (Psalm 139; Luke 1:15; Galatians 1:15) and of God's grace even preceding their conception (Jeremiah 1:5)—which casts light on the meaning of Gabriel's address to Mary as "favoured" and Elizabeth's declaration that she is "blessed among women" (Luke 1:28.42). Mary then accepted God's call to virginal motherhood in a graced assent for which she was enabled by God's prevenient preparation. In the Pauline perspective, she is emblematically "God's workmanship, created in Christ Jesus for good works which God prepared beforehand" (Ephesians 2:10). But all such graces are finally oriented to a destiny of glory (§54–5), which Scripture concretizes in Elijah (2 Kings 2:11), Enoch (Hebrews 11:5), and the penitent thief (Luke 23:43). For Mary, the disciple closest to Christ, it is most fitting that her union with God in life lead to her being gathered to God in death to share the new creation (§56–7).

Thus the Anglican and Catholic members of ARCIC arrive at affirming together as congruent with Scripture that God has taken Mary in her whole person into the fullness of glory, as the definition of 1950 stated—both in celebration of God's action in her and in effective demonstration of the destiny and the hope of all those joined in the communion of saints (§58). Moving from Mary's end back to her beginning, ARCIC acknowledges, in the light of Scripture, the reach of Christ's redemptive grace to fill Mary's life from her beginning, making her the prototype of a human being in which grace goes before any good action. This grace, however, is from the one Mediator who has ransomed all humans, whether they are touched and enlivened by his grace before or after he gave himself for all (§59).

To be more precise, ARCIC affirms the specifically Marian content of the dogma of the Assumption as being consonant with Scripture and with the ancient common tradition (§58), while the Immaculate Conception is "not contrary to the teaching of Scripture, and can only be understood in the light of Scripture" (§59). Both dogmas fit well with the biblical theology of grace and hope developed in *Mary: Grace and Hope in Christ*. Anglicans, however, must ask if these truths about Mary are revealed by God in a manner requiring those who profess the Church's Creed to hold them as well in faith. This question is raised in §60, leading to considerations of revelation, Scripture, and authoritative teaching in §61–3.

The papal documents that solemnly defined the Immaculate Conception and the Assumption cast these truths in the mold of propositions authoritatively issued as expressing particular contents of God's supernatural revelation. The definitions exemplify the account given by the First Vatican Council of truths belonging to the object of divine and

Catholic faith.[4] But today a new Catholic context of understanding surrounds Vatican I's account of revealed truths, situating differently the particulars of God's revelation, as the latter has been set forth in Vatican II's account of the word of God in the history of salvation. The culminating center of revelation is the life, death, and resurrection of Christ, which makes revelation preeminently salvific in its content and message.[5] God reveals himself as liberating us from sin and death and as raising us up to new life in Christ, in an economy of grace and hope, much as the Mary statement developed this.

The teaching authority is called to "preserve, expound, and disseminate" the saving word of God attested in Scripture and communicated by tradition (DV 9). It does not therefore announce new revelations but interprets the economy of salvation in Christ, that is, when with the help of the Holy Spirit "it listens to

---

4 "All those things are to be believed with divine and Catholic faith which are contained in the word of God, written or handed down, and which by the Church, either in solemn judgment or through her ordinary and universal teaching office, are proposed for belief as divinely revealed." Vatican II, *Dei Filius*, Ch. III; DH 3011, cited from J. Neuner & J. Dupuis, *The Christian Faith in the Doctrinal Documents of the Catholic Faith*, 7th edition, ed. J. Dupuis (Bangalore 2001), 45.

5 The whole Christ-event completes and perfects revelation, which in content manifests "that God is with us to deliver us from the darkness of sin and death, and to raise us up to eternal life" (*Dei Verbum* 4).

this devoutly, guards it reverently, and expounds it faithfully. All that it proposes for belief as being divinely revealed it draws from this sole deposit of faith" (DV 10). In the words of ARCIC, "the definitions are understood to bear witness to what has been revealed from the beginning" (§61). The obvious way to show that this is true in a given case is to examine the content of teaching in the framework of Scripture to test its congruence and homogeneity with the inspired, prophetic-apostolic, and authoritative biblical teaching – just as the Mary statement has done.

But here one can well recall how Catholics and Anglicans approach belief in Mary's Assumption and Immaculate Conception. ARCIC registers a positive appreciation of their Marian content when framed by the biblical context developed in §52–6. But for Catholics there is another dimension, different from an enhanced understanding of the meaning of the two doctrines. Catholics have *certainty* about the truth of the doctrines. This exemplifies what Vatican II said while treating Tradition and the Magisterium, namely, "the church does not draw its certainty about all revealed truths from Holy Scripture alone" (DV 9). The living tradition fostered growth in Catholic understanding of God's economy, and the

Papal Magisterium, in 1854 and 1950, defined the two truths as constitutive parts of this economy. Tradition and Magisterium interacted to give certainty about Marian contents of revelation.

When Anglicans question the binding character of the definitions of 1854 and 1950 because the Popes acted independently of a Council of the whole Church, Catholics point to the active support of the Catholic bishops, first in witnessing to convictions regarding the two truths held by the *sensus fidelium*, and then in re-affirming them at Vatican II (§62). But ARCIC also recognizes that post-Reformation controversy has disturbed perceptions on both sides of the place of Mary. Balance has been restored by Vatican II and presentations such as Pope Paul VI's *Marialis cultus* (1974), which hierarchize truths about Mary under the Incarnation and her role as *Theotókos*.

Today ARCIC looks to a common re-reception of Marian doctrine deepened by the eschatological perspective on our graced call and destiny, which features God's prevenient preparation for his service and then a personal renewal oriented to total sharing in Christ's glory. In such a framework, the Commission expresses the hope that the two bodies can recognize in each other's convictions genuine expressions of Christian faith, even though the same formulations are not used, namely, those of the definitions of 1854 and 1950, which however Anglicans would respect as legitimate.[6]

MARY IN THE DEVOTIONAL LIFE OF ANGLICANS AND CATHOLICS

In their lived religiosity, Anglicans have taken Mary principally as an exemplary disciple in responding life-long to God's call, while Catholic devotion features her ongoing role in the economy of salvation. But a shared basis, more evident in recent developments in both communities, is that Scripture and tradition set forth Mary "as the fullest human example of the life of grace", and consequently one to whom believers are called "to join with her as one indeed not dead, but truly alive in

---

6 §63, note 13, gives two precedents for a consensus in faith which admits ongoing differences in expression: (1) *The Common Christological Declaration between the Catholic Church and the Assyrian Church of the East* of 1994, which recognizes proper Christological faith, even where Mary is not addressed as *Theotókos* (Neuner-Dupuis, 7th ed., 277), and (2) the Lutheran-Catholic *Joint Declaration on the Doctrine of Justification* of 1999, which states a common conviction held in faith, but then analyses the two theological accounts of justification to show that the differences are not mutually exclusive and not destructive of the consensus in faith (Neuner-Dupuis, 844–52). But in both cases two existing bodies of doctrine were compared in considerable detail. Is there such a body of Marian doctrine among Anglicans to set into a dialogical relation with Catholic Marian teaching?

Christ" (§65). The principal link of Anglican and Catholic believers with Mary is in fact shared in the prayer of praise, both by praying her *Magnificat* and by explicitating our association with her in the communion of saints during our Eucharistic prayers.

The Reformation rejected an intercessory role for Mary because it threatened the unique and all-sufficient mediation of Christ and had no biblical basis, to which Catholic doctrine responded by reaffirming the long-standing practice of invoking her aid and, in Vatican II, placing her action not beside but within the unique action of her Son (LG 60).

The Mary statement moves ahead in §68–9 by reflecting on the incorporation of ecclesial ministries, rooted in Christ's mediation, in the application of salvation to believers. Scripture is also clear on believers requesting prayer and praying for each other in solidarity before God, which unfolds as mutual support in Christ empowered by the Holy Spirit. The natural extension of such requests to the departed saints "is not to be excluded as unscriptural, though it is not directly taught by the scriptures to be a required element of life in Christ" (§70). Naturally such petitions must not obscure that the help we seek comes indeed from the Father, through the Son our Highpriest, in the Holy Spirit.

The Mary statement approaches 'from below' the particularization of Mary's role in the communion of saints, by noting that many Christians are drawn to seek her help, e.g., by her intervention at Cana, and how they simply find her close to them in responding to God's call, in the poverty in which she gave birth, and in her suffering on Calvary. As she was mother of the Saviour, Christians have come to sense that she has an ongoing maternal concern in the unfolding of his redemptive work. Simply put, "Many Christians find that giving devotional expression to their appreciation for this ministry of Mary enriches their worship of God" (§73). ARCIC finds no reason to reject such devotion, while specifying that it should be a possible but not required practice.[7]

From its review of Mary's place, a different place and role in the devotional lives of Anglicans and Catholics, ARCIC concludes that the practice of asking Mary to pray to God for us should not divide our two communions.

The analysis in the Mary Statement of invoking Mary has led to a 'reconciled diversity' because, (1) what

7 The Lutheran theologian, Robert Jenson, approaches prayer for Mary's intercession from her divine motherhood, in "A Place for God", in *Mary, Mother of God*, eds Carl E. Bratten & Robert W. Jenson (Grand Rapids: Eerdmans 2004), 49-57.

Anglicans have feared to be intrinsic to Catholic devotion, that is, encroachment on Christ's atonement, is not the case, while Catholic fears of Anglican antipathy to Mary are also not verified. Also (2) the deeper concern of Anglicans to stress the sufficiency of Christ's salvation is not denied when Catholics stress how from Christ God empowers others as intercessors, nor do Anglican reservations about obligatory appeals to Mary entail a denial of the Catholic concern to feature the solidarity of the communion of saints.[8]

8 The analysis of "fears and concerns" became methodologically important in the reexamination by the German Ecumenical Working Group of the Reformation and Catholic mutual condemnations on the doctrine of justification. The result is the ascertaining of a basic compatibility, which was fundamental for the Lutheran-Catholic *Joint Declaration on the Doctrine of Justification* of 1999. For "Catholic doctrine does not overlook what Protestant theology stresses ... nor does it maintain what Protestant theology is afraid of ... Protestant theology does not overlook what Catholic doctrine stresses ... nor does it maintain what Catholic theology is afraid of ...". *The Condemnations of the Reformation Era. Do They Still Divide?* eds Karl Lehmann and Wolfhart Pannenberg (Minneapolis: Fortress 1990), 49. The nature and importance of this analysis of fears and deeper emphases is brought out in the study of the agreement on justification by Pawel Holc, *Un ampio consenso sulla dottrina della giustificazione* (Rome: Gregorian Univ. Press 1999), 145f, with reference as well to the Coptic-Catholic Christology study, and 244f. The same author shows the role of such an analysis in demonstrating the existence of a "differentiated consensus" between ecumenical partners, in "'Consenso differenziato' come categoria fondamentale nei dialoghi ecumenici", in *Sapere teologico e unità della fede*, Festschrift J. Wicks, eds. Carmen Aparicio et al. (Rome: Greorgian Univ. Press 2004), 434–50.

There is no need here to review the Conclusion of *Mary: Grace and Hope in Christ*, since the Anglican-Roman Catholic Commission does this succinctly but no less informatively in §78-9.

TWO PARTICULARS OF SPECIAL INTEREST

At least two characteristics of *Mary: Grace and Hope in Christ* make it unique among documents produced recently by bilateral ecumenical commissions. Its biblical interpretation goes in places beyond results of historical-critical interpretation to retrieve Mary's significance from Scriptural meanings that lie beyond the original communicative intent of the biblical author. This calls for notation and even critical review. Secondly, for its theological reflection on Mary's initial grace from God and her condition after death, ARCIC works creatively from an eschatological perspective given by a largely Pauline account of salvation entering our human lives.

SCRIPTURE IN THE LIGHT OF TRADITION

ARCIC states forthrightly that "our use of Scripture seeks to draw upon the whole tradition of the Church, in which rich and varied readings have been employed", and to integrate the valuable results of different approaches (§7). In fact the variety of 'readings' is said to be needed to correct imbalances arising from a single method: "typology can become extravagant, Reformation emphases reductionist, and critical methods overly historicist" (*Ibid.*).

The integration of results of different methods or 'readings' seems to presuppose achieving some degree of connection between them, so that the result is more than just a juxtaposition of the biblical narrative and different spiritual meanings of words, events, and persons.[9]

However, it must be said immediately that goodly portions of *Mary: Grace and Hope in Christ* elaborate quite soberly a biblical theology of God's dealings with his people and of Mary's role as Mother of the Messiah. Sobriety marks the accounts of Matthew 1–2 and Luke 1–2, with the latter being enriched in §15 by attention to how Gabriel's word about the Spirit "overshadowing" Mary echoes Septuagint terms describing the cherubim over the Ark (Exodus 25:20), God present over the Tabernacle (Exodus 40:35), and the brooding Spirit over the

---

9 The ecumenical approach to Mary with the methods of historical critical study, principally to retrieve the communicative intent of the biblical author in the setting of his original redaction, is fruitfully exemplified in *Mary in the New Testament*, eds Raymond E. Brown *et al.* (Philadelphia: Fortress & New York: Paulist, 1978), a study sponsored by the US Lutheran-Catholic dialogue.

waters (Genesis 1:2).[10] In receiving afresh the biblical witness, ARCIC laid hold of significant meanings without engaging in spiritual interpretation.

But on the Fourth Gospel in §22–7, sober narrative gives way to retrievals of symbolic meanings, beginning with the new wine of Cana, "symbolizing the eschatological marriage feast of God with his people and the messianic banquet of the Kingdom" (§23). "They have no wine" is taken as John's ascription to Mary of the messianic people's longing for salvation (§24), while her instruction "Do whatever he tells you" is the word of a believer now placed within the messianic community (§25). Similarly, the surface meaning of John 19:15–27 "invites a symbolic and ecclesial" reading of the narrative, in which Mary as "woman" is seen corporatively, or perhaps as the antitype of Eve, or "on a spiritual level" at the mother of all born anew of water and the Spirit (§26-7).

This commentator has written appreciatively of how the Groupe des Dombes situated its *relecture* of New Testament Marian texts in the framework of the

---

10 Perhaps a member of the Commission read the Greek of Luke 1:35 with a Septuagint concordance at hand, as was shown to be fruitful for Paul by the study of Richard B. Hays, *Echoes of Scripture in the Letters of Paul* (New Haven: Yale University Press 1989).

three articles of the Creed, thus relating Mary to the Creator, to the incarnate Son who came to glory in his resurrection, and to the Holy Spirit of Pentecost.[11] Since participants in bilateral dialogues work as representatives of their churches, their biblical work should be concerned to honour ways in which texts, in their history-of-effects, have been received by the communities of faith in ages past and present.[12] But the churches have also deemed necessary the work of disciplined recovery of the meanings that the biblical authors intended to communicate in the historical setting of the first redaction, which for a Catholic is easily recalled by mention of *Divino afflante Spiritu* (1943) and recent works by the Pontifical Biblical Commission.

Ecumenically fruitful biblical work is thus not easy when it seeks to respond to the two imperatives just

11 "The Virgin Mary in Recent Dialogues" (as in note 1), 37–40, where the resemblance was noted to the approach to Scripture proposed by George Lindbeck, in "Two Kinds of Ecumenism: Unitive and Interdenominational", *Gregorianum* 70 (1989), 647–60, at 657–9, and in "Scripture, Consensus, and Community", in R. J. Neuhaus, ed., *Biblical Interpretation in Crisis* (Grand Rapids: Eerdmans 1989), 74–101.

12 A recent essay shows the ecumenical fruitfulness of relating Mary to "the scriptural Christ" of the Church's faith, who is risen and exalted, as was proclaimed in the apostolic kerygma, and not to an allegedly historical Jesus lurking beyond hints given in our Gospels. David S. Yeago, "The Presence of Mary in the Mystery of the Church", in *Mary, Mother of God* (as in note 7), 58–79, at 59–63.

mentioned. The difficulty may have been felt by members of ARCIC. At any rate, the Commission seems not to have fully appropriated the symbolic meanings found in John 2 and 19, since the resumés of its biblical section, in §30 and the first part of §51, make no mention of symbols and types but remain almost totally within the framework of the sober gleanings from Luke. The Johannine paragraphs remain in the text, but the symbolic meanings found in them have not contributed substantially to the central doctrinal outcome of this phase of dialogue.

MARY IN THE GRACE AND HOPE OF THE ECONOMY OF SALVATION

One will ask just how ARCIC reached the significant conclusions of §58–9, which express agreement on Mary's Assumption and Immaculate Conception. The answer is found in §52–7, which articulate the "pattern of grace and hope" made manifest in Mary, but known from the development of this pattern in a central New Testament source, that is, a largely Pauline understanding of how salvation comes into human lives.

This commentator recommends that readers of §52–7 have the New Testament open before them for reading and pondering the many biblical passages to which these paragraphs refer as they weave their web of theological understanding concerning the economy of God's saving grace. These paragraphs are the hinge on which the argument of the document turns, as is indicated by taking the title of the whole from what is stated in §54: "This is the pattern of grace and hope which we see at work in the life of Mary."

The gain of this approach comes from prioritizing the perspective of the final destiny of graced human beings, that is, a consideration "in the light of what we are to become in Christ. ... We thus view the economy of grace from its fulfillment in Christ 'back' into history, rather than 'forward' from its beginning in fallen creation." (§52). Attention to this economy leads to a perception of the coherence of God's saving work, which is not fragmented into parts or elements simply juxtaposed. The future is especially relevant, for by faith, we are "a resurrection people" convinced of the present glory of Jesus Christ, with whom believers have become "joint heirs" (Romans 8:17) already raised with him (Ephesians 2:6; Colossians 3:1), as they were intended to be by God's choice before the foundation of the world (Ephesians 1:3–5).

There is thus a pattern of grace and hope in the unfolding economy. By grace believers, and particularly Mary, are "God's workmanship, created in Christ Jesus for good works which God prepared beforehand"

(Ephesians 2:10, cited in §55). God's intent goes before and his work anticipates what comes to be in history. As believers we live in hope, firmly based on the "first fruits of the Spirit", looking to "the redemption of our bodies" (Romans 8:23, referenced in §57), which was no less the well-grounded hope of Mary.

Thus ARCIC took what it calls an "eschatological perspective" (mentioned in §52, 54, 56, 59, and 63), to deepen its understanding of Mary by placing her in a horizon of truths expressed in New Testament letters which make hardly any mention of her. This is both to take Mary as "the fullest human example of the life of grace" (§65) and, methodologically, to operate from a conviction of the unity of the diverse New Testament works. Because the collection makes up a coherent whole, one can allow the letters to illumine the figure of Mary known principally from the Gospels.

The great gain of *Mary: Grace and Hope in Christ* thus comes by making fruitful for doctrinal understanding—and agreement—a biblical interpretation that is attentive to the "analogy of faith" as *Dei Verbum* recommended (DV 12.3).[13]

---

13 This term is often made obscure by attempts to explain it, but is best taken as referring to "the coherence of the truths of faith among themselves and within the whole plan of revelation" (*Catechism of the Catholic Church*, no. 114).

II. FURTHER CONSIDERATIONS OF SOURCES AND DOCTRINE FOR DIALOGUE ON MARY

Ongoing ecumenical exchanges on Marian doctrines and on Mary's place in prayer can, I want to suggest, be aided by further two considerations touched on but not extensively developed in *Mary: Grace and Hope in Christ.*

LITURGICAL SOURCES OF DOCTRINE AND MODELS OF DEVOTION

The recent Marian study of the Groupe des Dombes included the observation that the adage *Lex orandi [est] lex credendi* should not be applied to popular piety but to the official liturgical prayer of the church.[14] *Mary: Grace and Hope in Christ* agrees when it refers to Paul VI's insistence in *Marialis cultus* that the Christological focus of the Church's public prayer should give Marian devotion its proper location (§48) and ARCIC noted how recent Anglican additions of Marian feasts are significant because of the "definitive role of authorized liturgical texts and practices" for Anglicans (§49).

The Mary statement notes that liturgical forms of prayer involving the saints are not addressed to the

14 *Mary in the Plan of God* (as in note 1, above), 23 (no. 29).

saints as sources of grace and help, but to them as intercessors before God in gaining help to come from Him (§70). But more can be gleaned for dialogue from liturgical prayers said on Marian feast-days.

It can help in further dialogue of Catholics on Mary to keep in mind the themes actually expressed in the liturgical collects of the Marian feasts of the Roman Missal. A review of eleven such prayers, all addressed to God the Father, shows three thematic clusters concerning Mary.[15]

(1) On 1 January, both the regular and alternate collects invoke the *ongoing prayers of Mary*, asking that they may be always beneficial and be a source of joy for the people of the church, but this is asked in reference to her role in bringing us life and salvation through Jesus the Son whom she conceived and bore. The alternate collects of 25 March and of the evening of 14 August both ask that "the prayers of this woman [may] bring Jesus to the waiting world", while the regular collect of the latter formulary asks that her prayers may bring us to Christ's salvation

15 For 1 Jan., Mary Mother of God (regular and alternate collect); 25 Mar., the Annunciation (alternate); 31 May, the Visitation; evening of 14 Aug., Vigil of the Assumption (regular and alternate); 15 Aug. (regular and alternate); 8 Sept., Birth of Mary; 8 Dec., Immaculate Conception (regular and alternate collect). The initial collect for the Annunciation is focused on the Incarnation without mention of Mary.

and raise us to eternal life. A sixth collect, that of 8 December, moves to ask of God the Father, "Help us by her prayers to live in your presence without sin." – Mary, who lives among the redeemed, does pray for the world and for the church still *in via*.

(2) The collect of 8 September, for Mary's Nativity, moves directly to *petition God* with reference to both the birth of Jesus and Mary: "Father of mercy, give your people help and strength from heaven. The birth of the Virgin Mary's Son was the dawn of our salvation. May this celebration of her birthday bring us closer to lasting peace."

(3) In these collects, the more common form of petition is expressly theocentric. This appears in the subordination of a request of particular graces or helps to *what God effected in Mary* as commemorated on a given day. On 31 May, feast of the Visitation, which occasioned the *Magnificat*, the mention of God's inspiration of Mary to go to help Elizabeth leads to asking, "Keep us open to the working of your Spirit and with Mary may we praise you forever."

Both collects for the evening of 14 August speak of God's work in making Mary the mother of God's Son, with the regular collect adding God's crowning

her with glory, before asking that her prayers may
benefit the world and the church as indicated in (1)
above. The collects for the day of 15 August refer to
Mary's assumption into glory, which in the regular
prayer is God's work directly ("you raised ...") and
in the alternate collect God's work by a theological
passive ("she ... was raised ..."), before asking that
we may see heaven as our final goal (regular) or may
follow her example in reflecting God's holiness and
join her hymn of endless life and praise (alternate).[16]
On 8 December, the regular collect narrates God's
work ("You prepared ... let her share beforehand ...
kept her sinless") before asking that her prayers may
help us live without sin, while the alternate collect
of the Immaculate Conception offers the following
abundance of doctrine, narrative, and petition, with
even a connection with the Advent season in which
the feast falls:

Father, the image of the Virgin is found in the
Church. Mary had a faith that your Spirit prepared and a love that never knew sin, for you
kept her sinless from the first moment of her

16 The Mary statement saw this view in Pius XII's definition of the
Assumption: "We note that the dogma ... celebrates the action of God
in her" (§58).

conception. Trace in our actions the lines of her love, in our hearts her readiness of faith. Prepare once again a world for your Son who lives and reigns with you and the Holy Spirit, one God, for ever and ever. Amen.

These theocentric prayers of the Marian collects highlight God's initiative and the range of his work in the life and person of Mary. This, along with the previous two thematic clusters of the collects, can surely serve well in further Catholic contributions on Mary in ecumenical dialogues.

Mary's participated role in Christ

When the document *Mary: Grace and Hope in Christ* approaches Mary's intercession and mediation, it cites Vatican II's chapter on Mary: "Mary's maternal role towards the human race in no way obscures or diminishes the unique mediation of Christ, but rather shows its power" (LG 60, in §67). A similar affirmation follows shortly after, concerning ministries which mediate God's grace: "These ministries do not compete with the unique mediation of Christ, but rather serve it and have their source within it" (§68).

These statements call for further consideration of Christ the "one mediator between God and humankind,

... who gave himself a ransom for all" (1 Timothy
2:5), who then "was raised, who is at the right hand
of God, who indeed intercedes for us" (Romans
8:34).

Vatican II did open a further perspective on the Risen
Christ's saving mediation in the Marian chapter of
Lumen Gentium, in a dense text which incorporates
three steps. First, the Council states the uniqueness
of Christ. Then, it offers two comparisons which
suggest ways of understanding Christ's saving mediation, first, comparison with sharing in his priesthood, and, second, with the radiation of God's
goodness, which is *diffusivum sui*, throughout creation. Third, the same sentence affirms, concerning
Christ's saving work, a principle of *participation*, that
is, a sharing by others in their own way in what is
perfect in Christ. So we read in LG 62:

No creature could ever be counted along with
the Incarnate Word and Redeemer, but just as the
priesthood of Christ is shared (*participatur*) in
various ways by his ministers and people, and as
the one goodness of God is radiated in different
ways among his creatures, so also the unique
mediation of the Redeemer does not exclude
but rather gives rise to a manifold cooperation

which is but a sharing in one source (*suscitat variam ... participatam ex unico fonte cooperationem*).

The point is that Christ's unique, full, and perfect mediation is such that He actively transmits to others not only the benefits of his saving work but he also gives them a dependent and shared cooperation in his mediation. The grace of Christ radiates among God's human creatures first as redemptive from sin but also as transformative. It is *like-making*. Saving grace from Christ has as well the effect that Paul desired in believers, "Let the same mind be in you that was in Christ Jesus ..." (Philippians 2:5).

Here, we need to be reflectively aware of our own thought-forms. As persons wholly dependent for salvation on the work of Christ, we have to think and speak *dialectically*, being addressed by Paul, "what do you have that you did not receive? And if you received it, why do you boast as if it were not a gift?" (1 Corinthians 4:7). But once our dependence is thought through and made clear, we should not shy away from pondering the richness of the gift, where another thought-form can well be introduced, that of *participation*.

I am reminded of the remark of an astute Thomist of the Reformation era, when he responded to the

Protestant denial of the meritorious and satisfactory value of human graced good works. The opponents felt constrained to make this denial, lest they call in question the full and perfect sufficiency of the merit and satisfaction of Christ's death for us and for our salvation. The affirmation of Christ had to be guarded by a denial of a creaturely role. But the Thomist, Tommaso de Vio, Cardinal Cajetan, answered that ascribing meritorious value to the works of the justified does not come from holding an insufficiency on the side of Christ, but it is done instead precisely because of the singular richness of Christ's merit (*propter affluentiam*). For Christ gives his members a share in his merit, albeit in their order of dependent causes and in their partial and imperfect degree.[17] The key is not to think that a Yes to Christ means simply and solely a No to his members, dialectically, but to admit as well that Christ's influence extends

---

17 Cajetan, *De fide et operibus*, 12, translated in J. Wicks, *Cajetan Responds. A Reader in Reformation Controversy* (Washington: Catholic Univ. of America Press 1978), 237. The Thomist conviction is that created causes do not compete with God's universal causality. Human and divine agents are not a pair which divides the work, with each one's contribution delimiting that of the other. The creature does not supplement a weakness in God, nor does God's universal efficiency reduce the reality of created actions. It is instead a result of God's *abundantia* that he makes creatures active sharers in his own causality, as St Thomas explains in *Summa theologiae*, I, 22, 3.

to give others a mode of participation, on their level, in what he is and does.

Thus, Mary's intercession on behalf of the world is dependent on the unique and all-perfect mediation of her Son. It does not serve to supplement Christ's intercession, as if that needed completion. It is rather a manifestation of, or even a testimonial to, the supreme role of Christ that he incorporates others, preeminently his mother, into his ongoing intercession for the graces of his Spirit for us and for our salvation.

Thinking 'Thomisticly', to be sure, is not natural to many today, even to many Catholics, but in this Marian context, such thinking can surely be beneficial.

The Journey
An Anglican Perspective

Charles Sherlock

FACING ANGLICAN CHALLENGES

'Mother Church, mother Mary, mother mine'. This was
the watchword which I heard year by year as a child
on the fourth Sunday of Lent, Mothering Sunday.
I grew up in a series of Sydney parishes, and
Australian Anglicans thought of themselves very
much as members of the Church of England, continuing English customs.

Mothering Sunday gradually waned, but Mary continued to appear in Christmas pageants, and if you were
in church on Epiphany 2 (summer in Australia) when
John 2 was read, she may have been mentioned,
though holiday sermons more often took up the evils
of drink! *The Book of Common Prayer* (BCP) included
2 February and 25 March as major festivals, but few
parishes would observe such feasts unless they fell on
a Sunday. The focus for Presentation and Annunciation was the prophetic and angelic messages about
Christ rather than she to whom they came: I
cannot remember reflecting on 'full of grace' until

theological college. As regards Mary, that was about it —as a good Protestant I knew praying to anyone but God was pointless if not idolatrous. That Roman Catholics seemed to invoke Mary was another reason that they were only marginally Christian at best.

All this said, I have no memory of hearing anti-Mary sentiments in my evangelical upbringing, nor during my formative involvement in the Sydney University Evangelical Union. The virginal conception and birth of Christ arose quite often in discussion, but more in terms of biology, sex and ribaldry in the student newspaper than reflection on the 'virgin mother'. On the other hand, two Roman Catholic friends at university helped me realise that they could indeed be accepted as Christians, even if the doctrinal and devotional gap yawned wide (the Mass was then in Latin, and BCP reigned supreme among Anglicans).

Such a story is not untypical of many Anglicans approaching Mary: few polemics, but little positive teaching. Anglo-Catholics would have been more familiar with her place in Christian devotion, some observing not only the BCP festivals (birth of Mary, 8 September, conception of Mary, 8 December, and Visitation, 1 July as well as Presentation and Annunciation) but also 15 August (Assumption in the Western calendar).

CHALLENGES TO ANGLICANS

Perceptions gradually changed following the liturgical reforms which swept the English-speaking world from the 1960s, largely in the wake of Vatican II. That modern English became the language used in most churches of the English-speaking world made mutual understanding across Protestant-Roman Catholic lines much easier, and charismatic renewal helped many share in common spiritual experiences. In the process, controversy about the place of Mary in Christian faith and devotion largely died down, but underlying concerns remain among many Anglicans:

a) Is the Lord Jesus Christ really acknowledged by Roman Catholics as the "one mediator between God and humanity", both in official teaching and in devotional practice?

b) How does the affirmation of Mary as 'full of grace' relate to the scriptural truth that we are saved only by the grace of Christ, given by divine initiative through the Spirit?

c) Are the two distinctively Roman Catholic dogmas, Immaculate Conception and Bodily Assumption, sufficiently supported by the Scriptures?

d) These dogmas are the only examples of the Bishop of Rome defining a doctrine as infallible: what does this say about his exercise of authority?

e) Given that these dogmas, as infallible truths, have been declared to be binding on all the faithful, what might this mean for Anglicans in a future union of the churches?

f) How does the teaching embedded in these dogmas engage with the exercise of reason, for example the role of historical analysis, and the relation of body and soul in anthropology?

g) Can the ideal for women of Mary as 'virgin mother', regarded today as spiritually damaging by many Anglicans, be redeemed to bring Mary into focus as a contemporary image of healthy Christian discipleship?

h) ARCIC has sought to face and respond to these concerns, and find positive ways forward by which Roman Catholics and Anglicans (and other Christian traditions of both East and West) may together recover authentic teaching and devotion. Some have been taken up in earlier work, as noted in the early sections of *Mary: Grace and Hope in Christ*. Thus mediation is addressed in *Authority in the Church II* (1981—see *Mary* §2 and Section D). The authority of the Bishop of Rome to define faith is taken up in *The Gift of Authority: Authority in the Church III* (1998), and its consequence, the binding nature of dogmas, is discussed in *Mary* §61–3. The remaining concerns—grace, the Scriptures, the place of reason, feminist insights—are addressed throughout the Statement, though only to the extent that they are matters which divide Roman Catholics and Anglicans.

Whether or not this Agreed Statement meets Anglicans' expectations, and whether its conclusions are received positively by the Anglican Communion, is not for this paper to say: it seeks to show how Anglican members of the Commission contributed to the formulation of this Statement, and subsequently signed off on it. Part A outlines its development from an Anglican perspective; Part B offers an 'Anglican commentary'. But first, a personal aside.

A PERSONAL ASIDE

This paper arises from personal experience in ARCIC, as probably the most 'protestant' member of the Commission. When asked in 1991 to join the Commission, I realised that to accept the invitation with integrity required commitment to the goal of full, visible communion, and to the ARCIC method: getting behind entrenched positions to formulations which could open up the future. The invitation was not accepted lightly, but in the spirit of seeking to work towards positive, authentic outcomes rather than defending the *status quo*.

Working along these lines was relatively easy in our work on morals (*Life in Christ*, 1994), harder on authority (*The Gift of Authority*, 1998), but tested severely on Mary. My spiritual journey had little place for Mary, and none for invocation, not only from lack of experience but also for positive reasons. Further, Jean-Marie Tillard was to take no part in this work: his approach to church and theology, grounded in grace, vision and the discipline of true freedom, had given me hope when no way forward seemed open, and he understood Anglicans of evangelical conviction. Thirdly, when I became a member of the drafting team it meant not only responding to what others had written, but being part of originating the argument. This said, I stand behind *Mary: Grace and Hope in Christ* with enthusiasm, believing that it is in accordance with the Scriptures, and consonant with the 39 Articles and Anglican formularies. I am persuaded that its acceptance will advance the Gospel of Jesus Christ both among God's people, and in the wider world. At the conclusion of our work in Seattle each member signed a copy of the Statement: I did so in good conscience, and gladly.

Other Commission members would tell the story differently: each comes from a distinct ecclesial context and varied devotional practice, and senses particular audiences looking on 'over the shoulder'. For myself, these audiences included Anglicans of evangelical conviction, other evangelicals and Protestants in Australia, including the Baptist, Churches of Christ, Salvation Army and Uniting traditions, and the pragmatic egalitarian ethos of ordinary Australians. How the Statement would be read by others, notably Anglo-Catholic Anglicans, I could not anticipate, but it seems to have evoked the reaction 'this enables us to live truths we hold dear, in ways which other Christians can join', rather than 'we were right all along'.

A   THE DEVELOPMENT OF THE STATEMENT

ARCIC members came to the 1998 meeting in Rome to conclude *The Gift of Authority*, unsure of what future lay beyond this. We were informed that a gathering was planned for 2000 of pairs of Anglican and Roman Catholic bishops from places where both traditions live together, to consider how ARCIC's work might be taken further in practical terms. In 1999 we would assist with the preparation —and commence work on Mary. There was reticence about this latter task, since the main issues would seem to have been addressed in *Authority in the Church II* and *The Gift of Authority*. Further, the sheer volume of possible topics, many best left in their historical resting-places, was daunting. Conversely, the need to address the theological significance of popular devotion, and reactions to it, was acknowledged.

1999 (MISSISSAUGA): LISTENING AND LEARNING

So in August 1999 the Commission met at a retreat centre in Mississauga, Canada, to plan for the 2000 gathering, to consider initial responses to *The Gift of Authority* (published in early 1999), and to start work on Mary.

On Mary, a contribution from Jean-Marie Tillard was first considered. This advocated approaching the dogmas as 'mythological' expressions of revealed truth, but a consensus emerged that this was unhelpful in addressing the communion-dividing issues. As it turned out, Jean was to take no further (earthly) part in the Commission. Several other articles were considered, including one from Rowan Williams (not then Cantuar), and papers presented by two external scholars, one addressing Mary in the Anglican tradition, the other summarizing ecumenical resources for the study. My learning from these discussions was that Mary was more than just another disciple, but stood in a distinctive relationship to Christ. And I remember causing a stir at one point (not least to the Anglican co-chair) by referring to Mary as a 'sinner', not realizing the issues involved.

Two practical steps were taken: topics were identified for specific work, with ten papers commissioned from Commission members, and a draft schema was drawn up. The schema situated the topic in the light of *The Gift of Authority*: while different to the eventual Statement, a significant note says "the main emphasis will be on Mary in relation to Christ and the Church, but issues of Christian anthropology may be included, with sensitivity, at certain appropriate points". This agreement followed discussion of feminist insights, and how they might assist the work. John Muddiman had contributed a paper, and the ARCUSA Statement, *Images of God: Reflections on Christian Anthropology*, had been considered. The Commission concluded that these topics, and the emphases in the *Magnificat* on justice and empowerment, were not matters of division between us, so did not properly fall within our brief. On the other hand, their omission from the Statement would leave a significant lacuna and lead to misunderstanding: they are addressed, if briefly, in *Mary* §71–4.

Further, care came to be taken with 'mother' language—including avoidance of 'Mother of God', which misleads many English speakers—and the way in which women's experience is taken up in the Statement.

2000 (PARIS): SURPRISES AND FOUNDATIONS

2000 saw the Commission meet in a convent adjacent to Sacré Coeur in the village of Montmartre, working through the commissioned papers. Brief papers were written during the meeting by our Scripture scholars, John Muddiman (Anglican) and Adelbert Denaux (Roman Catholic)—e.g., on 'Ephesians 2:3 and Original Sin'. These specific contributions proved to be valuable as work progressed, keeping us honest in using the scriptures. Of particular importance for me was their work on typology, Mary's family and Romans 3.23 (cf. footnotes 1, 3 and 12).

The prepared papers offered some surprises, notably Nicholas Sagovsky and Michael Nazir-Ali showing the English Reformers' acceptance of the perpetual virginity of Mary, and their reticence (along with Hooker) about her status as a sinner. This paper led us to read Cranmer (and his sources in Augustine) carefully, and to reflect more deeply on Christ's atonement in relation to his mother. Another paper showed that England's eastern counties were the fountain-head of extreme Marian devotion in the fourteenth century, and consequent iconoclasm in the sixteenth—Mariolatry was not a continental importation, but the reverse was rather the case.

Several papers underscored the need to ground the issues in a strong understanding of grace, and clear away wrong perceptions on this score (notably Liam Walsh on original sin). Sara Butler helped Anglicans appreciate Vatican II on Mary, especially the significance of the decision not to prepare a separate Constitution on Mary but include her in *Lumen Gentium*. Jaci Maraschin on 'Mary in Brazilian popular devotion' considered the interaction of traditional religious figures and Mary, complemented by an (external) paper from Eamon Duffy. The paper which affected me most, however, was that prepared by Peter Cross and myself (building on AustARC's *The Saints and Christian Prayer*). It noted the relative absence of eschatology in ARCIC's work thus far, took up the language of the saints in Christ as 'truly alive', and advocated doing theology from the 'future backwards'. Combined with discussion of Romans 8:27–30, this was to become a major 'engine' for the work on Mary.

This Paris meeting saw an 'Emerging Shape of the

ARCIC Study on Mary drafted, identifying topics to be included. It recommends "a document with a doxological/liturgical tone", and notes that "an organizing motif might be the Romans 8.30 scheme: calling, justifying, sanctifying, glorifying". The Statement needs to be "situated in the light of the Trinity", and an outline for a New Testament section is included, with sections on the 'common tradition', noting themes such as "perpetual virginity, sinlessness of Mary, *panagia*, dormition", and one considering "Mary in the liturgical life of contemporary Anglicans and Catholics". This outline concludes with the question, "What do we want to say about the dogmatic definitions in the light of the above?", revealing the inconclusive nature of discussion thus far.

Further papers were sought: exegesis of the two Marian dogmas and the context for their promulgation (Sara Butler and Liam Walsh); the English Reformation (Nicholas Sagovsky and Michael Nazir Ali); contemporary liturgical provisions (Peter Cross and Charles Sherlock); and the patristic period viewed from Eastern and Western perspectives (Emmanuel Lanne). It was becoming clear that this Statement was going to take longer than originally envisaged, that a focus to bring it together was needed, and that a Pauline approach might be that focus.

2001 (DUBLIN): A THEME EMERGES

The Church of Ireland Teaching Training College, Dublin, was the venue for the 2001 meeting. It commenced with the commissioned papers: much clarity was gained from their precision, particularly on the patristic period, and the texts of the dogmas. Close attention was then paid to a draft of 'Mary in the Scriptures' prepared by the Scripture scholars, including the issue of typology. A further outline was prepared, now with seven sections. Those on the Scriptures and the early Church existed in draft form, but sections on 're-receptions of the faith we share', 'Mary and the life of grace (Romans 8:30)' and the dogmas, and 'Mary in the life of the Church' were but sketches. Agreement was reached on the scriptural data on Mary, on her significance as *Theotókos*, and our being open to 're-receiving' the dogmas, but the Commission was struggling to move forward.

My learning from this work was that Anglicans tend to see Mary as a wonderful example from the past, whereas Roman Catholics experience her as a living presence. Do we sing *Magnificat* because Mary sang it once, or sing it with her now? I came to realize that her (incontrovertible) status as *Theotókos* was a present as well as a past reality, since she is 'truly alive': this realization assists greatly in appreciation of Mary's distinctive place among the people of God.

2002A (CHEVETOGNE): ESCHATOLOGICAL EXCITEMENT

Against this background, the co-chairs set up a drafting group to bring together the materials gathered, develop the Romans 8:30 approach, and bring a fresh draft to the 2002 meeting in Vienna. Adelbert Denaux, Sara Butler, Nicholas Sagovsky and myself met for five intense (and cold!) days in January 2002 at the Benedictine monastery of Chevetogne in Belgium, where Emmanuel Lanne is a member, and which encompasses monks from Eastern as well as Western rites. A full draft of the present Sections A —C resulted, driven by seeing things from the future backwards, rather than from the past forwards.

In particular, a 'reversal' of Romans 8:30—glorified, justified, called, predestined—was used to set Mary within a 'Pauline' framework, with texts such as Colossians 1:27 and especially Ephesians 2:8–10 coming to have a striking new light for us. Mary was thus acknowledged in the first place as a corporate rather than individual figure, which marked a significant breakthrough in the thinking of Nicholas and myself. It enabled the team as a whole to agree on

Mary's place in the 'economy of hope and grace' (a phrase summing up this approach), and apply this to the dogmas, assisted by detailed attention to the definitive Latin texts. Approaches to Mary grounded in election, the Annunciation, or just history, began from the 'past', and raised difficulties, not least that this was unavoidably in thrall to sin: where might an approach from the 'future' lead us?

To my mind these days were the decisive 'moment' in the work on Mary, and the 'eschatological' motif is the key for Anglicans especially to understand the agreement reached.

2002B (VIENNA): CONSOLIDATION AND PROGRESS

The 2002 ARCIC meeting in Vienna (at a Focolare centre) opened with two days' strong discussion of the new draft paragraph by paragraph: it was warmly affirmed, with some modifications suggested, most notably in the ways in which the dogmas were handled.

The Commission divided into four pairs to work on the drafted material, accompanied by one drafter each. I was assigned to the group drafting Section D, invocation and mediation: we drew on work done by AustARC in 1996–99 on *The Saints and Christian Prayer*. The overall outcome was a tighter draft in the scriptural area, a reshaping of the historical/

theological section (including a close discussion of *Sub tuum praesidium* based on the Greek text, cf. footnote 9), and general approval of the work on invocation/mediation. The eschatological theme was to my mind somewhat dimmed, but not quenched: it remained to be seen whether the drafters' approach to the dogmas would commend itself when worked out fully.

More generally, the experience of reading the scriptures *together* across the Protestant/Catholic divide was coming to take on considerable significance. The careful work done by our Scripture scholars on the 'obvious' Mary passages arose from the tools of academic scholarship, but gradually the importance of disciplined imagination ('typology') came into play, and the introduction of Pauline texts into the picture drove us to more deliberately 'theological' reading, now being done ecclesially—*together*.

2002C (CHEVETOGNE): THE DOGMAS IN FOCUS

The drafting group took up the reins in a second meeting at Chevetogne in November 2002. The history section was brought together as one section, and discussion of the dogmas was brought into close relationship to the eschatological motif.

Both Anglican drafters were by now convinced that this

reading of the dogmas expressed the profound scriptural truth that God's grace not only 'goes before' in salvation, but 'reaches back' to transform this old creation into the new — and that Mary is rightly seen as embodying this hope.

2003 (FLORIDA): ALMOST THERE

The Commission's 2003 meeting, at an Anglican retreat centre in Florida, was spent in solid work on what is now Section C: discussion of the dogmas in the order Assumption *then* Immaculate Conception retained the eschatological theme. Given that work had been in progress for five years, there was pressure to finish, but the issues around the dogmas as binding (*de fide*) remained, and the drafters believed that ARCIC's traditional paragraph by paragraph vote on a Statement could not be short-circuited. And there was still no definitive title!

2004 (SEATTLE): EARTHQUAKES SURVIVED

A 'half-meeting' was organized for Seattle in late January 2004, timed to precede the scheduled meeting of the International Anglican-Roman Catholic Commission on Unity and Mission (IARCCUM), and to enable the Commission to hand over its work on the feast of the Presentation

(2 February). This meeting turned out to be quite a dramatic time – we lost our co-chair, received a heart-withering critique, but finally gained a title.

Since the Florida meeting, the ECUSA General Convention had voted to confirm the consecration of a priest living in a same-sex relationship, and Frank Griswold, ARCIC co-chair since 1999, participated as ECUSA Presiding Bishop. He subsequently stood down as ARCIC co-chair, being replaced by IARCCUM member Peter Carnley, Primate of the Anglican Church of Australia. The Vatican had asked that the meetings of the full Commission of IARCCUM be put on hold (it has now resumed) but agreed that ARCIC should proceed. Over five full days the Statement was concluded: on subscription to the dogmas, precedents from the Assyrian Church of the East—Roman Catholic dialogue were employed.

A different matter dominated the opening days. Comments had been sought by the secretaries from selected readers before the Florida meeting, and these had been very helpful. The near-final Florida draft had then been referred to an Anglican scholar with the idea of a Commentary being prepared in good time. His response, however, reflected the sharpest edge of Protestantism. Given the academic, ecclesial and spiritual respect in which he was held, working through this critique was extremely painful for the two Anglican drafters. Nevertheless, his critique led to a thorough review of the Statement, in particular the eschatological motif. The outcome was the correction of some errors, and some improvements, but the shape and content of the document stood. One personal disappointment was the omission (from §52) of reference to Mary as *panagia*, translated 'holy through and through', a positive expression of her unique status in Christ.

The last twist of this final meeting, however, was finding a title for the Statement. Several had been suggested over the years, with general agreement that 'Mary' should be the first word, and that 'Christ' must appear prominently. 'Grace' and 'hope' had become increasingly prominent in the work, but only in the last minutes available was 'Mary: Grace and Hope in Christ' proposed, and immediately accepted. Each member signed sufficient copies for each to receive an autographed one.

ARCIC concluded its work that afternoon with a memorable Vespers for the feast of the Presentation, including a sermon from Nicholas Sagovsky – a good way to end, even if we were unable to hand over our work formally to IARCCUM.

LOOKING FORWARD, LOOKING BACK

The key shift in this journey was reframing our understanding of Mary in Pauline terms. Discussion of the Scriptures directly referring to Mary had produced agreement, but not enabled us to come to grips with the dogmas, nor connected adequately with the patristic emphasis on her as a corporate, typological figure. Paul may say nothing directly about Mary, but understands humanity in fundamentally corporate and eschatological terms (cf. Romans 5 and 1 Corinthians 15 especially). Bringing together these two approaches (Sections A and C), bridged by careful reflection on the tradition (Section B), is thus the fundamental structure of the Statement, issuing in agreement about the place of Mary in the life of the Church (Section D).

B AN ANGLICAN COMMENTARY

Mary: Grace and Hope in Christ represents a further development of themes opened up in *The Gift of Authority*, as might be expected, since the dogmas about Mary represent the only examples of the exercise of the Bishop of Rome's distinctive authority. These matters are taken up, but the Statement's most notable features lie elsewhere, in its surprises of method, theme and ethos.

METHOD: THE IMPORTANCE OF HOPE

The method which ARCIC has followed from its inception has been to 'get behind' polemical formularies, to explore the faith which Anglicans and Roman Catholics (and other Christians) share, in such a way that differences may be seen in new ways. The fruit of such a method is seen in *The Final Report* (1982, covering Eucharist, Ministry and Authority), and in *Salvation and the Church* (1987). In these Statements the Commission generally came to conclusions of positive agreement, along with acknowledging unresolved areas (including the dogmas about Mary).

Church as Communion (1991) varied this method in two main ways: its subject matter was not controverted, so 'getting behind' was less relevant, and opportunity was taken to harvest the insights gained from understanding 'church' in terms of *koinonia*.

With *Life in Christ: Morals, Communion and the Church* (1994), ARCIC resumed the 'get behind the past' method, though finding it necessary to write at greater length and in more detail due to the subject matter. This more descriptive method also led to the conclusion reached being 'double negative' rather than positive: the differences which would remain, were the approach taken in the Statement adopted by the churches, would not of themselves constitute a barrier to communion. By now it would seem that the 'get behind' method was starting to reveal its limits. In particular, it oriented discussion to the past, from which approach some topics would remain intractable. This is recognized to some extent in *The Gift of Authority*, in which hints of a 'future into the present' orientation emerge in the discussion of 'tradition', complementing the 'past into the present' one.

This eschatological orientation comes to the fore in *Mary: Grace and Hope in Christ* (as the title implies). The document is laid out on 'traditional' ARCIC lines, with the canonical Scriptures considered first, then historical issues taken up ('past to present'). But it is evident that this writing is itself the fruit of a significant 'future to present' re-reading of the canonical Tradition and historical traditions. When it comes to the theological content of the Church's teaching about Mary, the eschatological balance to the 'get behind' method comes to full flower, in ways that offer significant challenges to all Christians, not least Anglicans. In the process, Protestant and Enlightenment concerns are addressed, and insights from the Eastern Christian tradition are sensitively harvested: this illustrates the importance for wider ecumenical ecclesiological reflection of integrating 'past' and 'future' beginnings to our learning in the present.

METHOD: THE CENTRALITY OF GRACE

As noted, the theological significance of Mary is discussed in terms of 'Pauline' categories rather than those of the evangelists, Luke in particular, as has traditionally been the case. Such an approach begins from the vision of redeemed humanity in Christ, in which we participate now by faith, then 'face to face' (a favourite theme in Augustine). Mary, who remains uniquely in relation to the One she bore in her own flesh, is understood as the fulfilment in human terms of the hope we have in Christ, a hope which reached 'backward' in her own life to the fullest extent.

This way of re-expressing the theological teaching of the Assumption and Immaculate Conception may appear forced or fanciful to some readers. If it does represent a faithful re-reading of the Roman Catholic Church's teaching about God's work in and through Mary, however, it offers a significant opportunity to bear witness to the truth about what it means to be human in today's world. The Commission claims that its approach in no way compromises the unique saving work of Christ, our utter reliance on the Spirit, nor the centrality of grace in redemption. It does point up the way in which humanity actively participates in the divine work of recreation, of which Mary is a unique paradigm.

This approach also represents a significant development of the 'Yes/Amen' motif in *Gift*: it is paradigmatic of the Annunciation narrative, with its implicit theology of grace (cf. §16) and of the Christian life (§64). The Commission worked hard in reviewing the historical development of reflection upon Mary, the debates about original sin, 'moments' of conception, the maculist and other controversies which lay behind the Reformation differences about grace and sin. Yet—following on its earlier work—the Commission affirms a clear unanimity about the fundamental issues involved, especially as seen in terms of the redeeming and renovating work of Christ and the Spirit. This approach is of particular significance to Christians concerned about Mary displacing Christ in the divine pattern of grace: situating the discussion in a 'Pauline' framework brings surprises, but forms a convincing re-orientation which illuminates much of the tradition in unexpected ways.

MARY AND SPIRITUALITY: FAITH AND SIGHT

This 'Pauline' approach can lead to unexpected exegesis (e.g., of Ephesians 2:8–10) which some readers may question. But it has the distinct advantage of coming to see Mary in the first place—that is, 'by faith'—in terms of our corporate (redeemed) humanity, rather than as a particular individual viewed through the lens of historical research—that is, 'by sight'. The Statement thus seeks not to reconcile 'liberal/Enlightenment' perspectives with 'traditional/ dogmatic' ones, but to fold them together, just as a healthy ecclesiology refuses to let go of seeing the Church both through the eyes of 'faith' (as confessed in the Creeds) and of 'sight' (the lived reality of Church which we experience, as acknowledged in Reformation confessions such as Articles 19–21).

Such a reconciliation would only seem possible as we approach theology as Christian spirituality. The Commission's spiritual experience of living in varied houses of prayer, its common life of prayer, reflection on the Scriptures and sharing of the Ministry of the Word in the eucharist, played major roles in its work on Mary. This spirituality can be seen in the scrupulous, elegant and challenging reflection on biblical data in the early paragraphs, and the illuminating discussion of invocation of the saints in the final sections, which are the result of common experience of prayer in communion. When Mary is viewed in the first place in corporate terms, as 'type' of the Church, embodying its full purity as the one in the closest communion with its Saviour and Head, invoking her could be understood as a personal way of asking for the prayers of the Church as a whole—an idea with profound possibilities for the reconciliation of clashing spiritualities.

ACCORDING TO THE SCRIPTURES?

How, then, are 'ordinary' Anglicans likely to receive this Statement? Much will depend on the extent to which its method is appreciated. It represents a major shift of perspective for most Anglicans, and probably more than any previous work of ARCIC needs to be read in the light of the method by which it has been prepared. Readers who assume that the Commission works from past to present to negotiate a compromise 'deal' acceptable to 'the Anglican view' will reject it, and harshly, because the positive gains which the Statement claims will of necessity be seen as 'giving in to Rome'.

The most significant issue for most Anglican readers is the extent to which the Statement allows them to consider seriously whether its conclusions are 'according to the Scriptures'. This applies not only to those who accept the description of conservative evangelical, but to the overwhelming majority of the Communion for whom the two dogmas are frequently dismissed as impossible to reconcile with Scripture, let alone reason. The Commission has sought to read the Scriptures together, employing a disciplined use of typology to honour the text, respect critical approaches to it, and keep the primary context of shared spirituality to the fore. Many Anglicans long to explore deeper ways into their relationship with God and one another in Christ: this Statement may offer a fruitful way in which such longings can find home, in fuller ecumenical *koinonia*.

MARY: THE EVANGELICAL ELEMENT

Beyond questions about scriptural foundation, however, many Anglicans will want to know what there is about the *gospel* in this Agreement. It is one thing to remove obstacles in such a fraught area, another to move readers to a positive approach.

The gospel proclaims God's redemptive work in Christ, rescuing us *from* death, sin and all the consequences of rebelling against our maker. Often, however, the positive note of what we are saved *for*—what we are to be and become—is more muted. To view Mary, by faith, participating in the fullness of human destiny in Christ, offers a fresh sense of gospel hope to humankind—in this way she is indeed pattern of 'grace and hope in Christ'.

The Mary Statement
A Roman Catholic Perspective

Sara Butler

THE AGREED STATEMENT AND THE DOGMATIC DEFINITIONS

In the Agreed Statement, *Mary: Grace and Hope in Christ*, ARCIC investigates two doctrines that were formally defined in the Roman Catholic Church after the sixteenth century breach in communion, the Immaculate Conception and the Assumption of the Blessed Virgin Mary. These 'Marian dogmas' are a stumbling block in the path of reconciliation because Roman Catholics not only believe what they teach, but are in fact obliged to believe them, whereas Anglicans traditionally make no commitment to them and are free to reject them.

The truths defined are not central to Christian faith like the Trinity, the Incarnation, and the Redemption; they do not rank high in the 'hierarchy' of truths to be believed. It might seem, then, that there is no need to reach an ecumenical consensus on them. The doctrines were not officially proposed as belonging to the deposit of faith until rather recently (1854 and 1950), and they were defined in order to confirm beliefs about Mary's origins and final destiny, not to defend a truth that was under attack. On the other hand, Roman Catholics have celebrated the feasts of Mary's Conception and Assumption for hundreds of years (since the seventh century for the first and the sixth century for the second); the beliefs associated with them are enshrined in our litanies and our hymns, our iconography and our corporate imagination. They have become integral to our understanding of Mary's office as the Mother of God.

Until the Reformation these feasts were celebrated throughout England. During the controversies of the sixteenth century, however, the Roman Church was accused of exalting Mary at the expense of her Son (§44). The English Reformers, after testing the Church's belief and practice against the Scriptures and the ancient Christian traditions, removed the feast of Mary's Assumption as 'unscriptural' and liable to detract from the unique dignity of the Saviour. They retained the feast of her Conception, but held that she, like the rest of us, was in need of a Redeemer (§46). Anglican theologians did not participate in the development that led up to the two papal definitions. Today, they continue to question their foundation in the Scriptures, and to raise objections about the manner by which they were defined, that is, by a pope independent of a council (§2).

ARCIC believes that its exposition of these truths, "understood within the biblical pattern of the economy of hope and grace", affords a sufficient basis for reconciliation, with respect to the content of the dogmas (§60, 78). Roman Catholics readers of *Mary: Grace and Hope in Christ* will naturally want to be assured that the Agreed Statement faithfully attests to the truths proposed in these dogmas. This essay will focus on this concern. It hopes to show that the consensus reached by ARCIC reproduces, although in somewhat different terms and from a different perspective (§63, note 13), the doctrines of Mary's Immaculate Conception and Assumption that Roman Catholics profess. We shall take note of some features common to the two doctrines and then examine each of the papal definitions.

SOME FEATURES COMMON TO THE TWO DOCTRINES

In 1854, Pope Pius IX solemnly defined the Church's belief that Our Lady was conceived without original sin. Almost one hundred years later, in 1950, Pope Pius XII solemnly defined the Church's belief that at the end of her life Mary was assumed body and soul into heavenly glory. The two definitions are unusual not only by reason of the manner of their definition, but also by reason of the warrants for their content. The magisterium offers scriptural testimony to these beliefs, but the real warrant seems to be "ecclesial practice" (the celebration of the feasts) or even the *sensus fidelium*, that is, the intuition of faith by which the Roman Catholic faithful actually hold these doctrines as true.[1] Although they follow from biblical revelation and can be understood only in light of it, these beliefs are not directly enunciated in the Scriptures. Apart from the Tradition, then, their foundation in Sacred Scripture is difficult — if not impossible — to discover. They emerged in the Church's consciousness only gradually, as the fruit of Christian devotion and contemplation.[2] They follow from the logic of love. What the judgement of the magisterium ultimately confirms is the conviction of the faithful, supported by the unanimous teaching of the bishops, regarding both of these truths concerning Mary. By means of papal definitions, these doctrines

1 In its Agreed Statement, *The Gift of Authority* (1999), §29, 36, 43, ARCIC examines the interplay between the *sensus fidelium* and the *magisterium* of the bishops.
2 The place of the *sensus fidelium* in the development of dogma is identified in *Dei Verbum* 8.

are infallibly proposed as "divinely revealed" truths, truths that belong to the apostolic faith.

The doctrines themselves have to do with the triumph of God's grace in Mary, the Mother of the Saviour; they elude historical investigation and proof. They were defined as true because they were believed, just as they were celebrated because they were believed.[3] Prior to the papal definitions, this 'sense of the faithful' had been officially confirmed by means of the episcopal and then papal approval given to the liturgical celebration of Mary's Conception on 8 December (in the East, 9 December) and her Assumption on 15 August. In each case, permission to celebrate these feasts, plus the explicit approval of liturgical texts for them, required a formal intervention of the magisterium. Here we see how the 'law of prayer is the law of belief'.

The 'fundamental principle' of Marian doctrine, according to the common teaching of Roman Catholic theologians, is Mary's office as *Theotókos*, "Mother of God Incarnate". All subsequent doctrinal elaborations have arisen from reflection on the uniquely privileged relationship between this mother and this Son.

---

3 Their chief function is 'doxological', that is, they express the Church's praise of God for what he has done for Mary. See Joseph Cardinal Ratzinger, *Daughter Zion: Meditations on the Church's Marian Belief* (San Francisco: Ignatius Press, 1983), 73.

Such is clearly the case with these two dogmas. According to the first, God preserved Mary from all stain of original sin so that she could, in perfect freedom, utter her *fiat*. According to the second, God assumed Mary, body and soul, into heavenly glory at the end of her life so that she could share fully, even now, in her Son's victory. Both of these Marian privileges arise from her relationship to Christ. It was in view of his merits that Mary was preserved from all stain of original sin; and it is because of her intimate bodily relation with him as God-bearer that she has been taken into his heavenly glory. Another, rather simple, way of stating both the Christological and soteriological dimension of these doctrines is to say that Christ shares with his mother his victory over sin and death: over sin—the Immaculate Conception; over death—the Assumption.[4] Thus, Mary is perfectly redeemed; the grace of Christ is completely victorious in her.

What is the precise content of the definitions proposed in the papal definitions? While the two dogmas form a kind of pair, for this next step we need to examine each one individually, and point to where ARCIC's proposal corresponds to them.

---

4 This formulation is found twice in the apostolic constitution of Pius XII on the Assumption, *Munificentissimus Deus*, arts. 4 and 39.

THE IMMACULATE CONCEPTION

The dogma of the Immaculate Conception, taken positively, is an affirmation and celebration of Our Lady's holiness.[5] It affirms that Mary was thoroughly holy, by God's grace, from the first moment of her conception. The actual text of the papal definition (see §59), however, is framed rather differently. Pope Pius IX speaks not of Mary's holiness but of her 'sinlessness', in fact, of her 'preservation' from sin - *original* sin. He asserts that God prepared the Virgin Mary for her unique role in a unique way, namely, by preserving her from all 'stain' of original sin. God's grace shielded Mary from the contagion of Adam's sin from the first moment of her conception, and this 'singular grace and privilege' was given her in view of the merits of her Son, 'the Saviour of the human race'. Mary could truly sing that God was her "Saviour" (Luke 1:47).

To understand why the doctrine of Mary's 'all-holiness' was formulated in terms of preservation from original sin rather than fullness of grace, it is necessary to know something of its history. This history also helps to explain why it came to be defined. Although this doctrine was not defined in order to suppress a

5 See *Catechism of the Catholic Church (CCC)*, §490–3.

heresy, its definition did serve to consolidate and confirm the Church's faith after a prolonged and rather bitter struggle, in the West, over whether Mary's sinlessness included freedom even from original sin. What simple believers grasped with the sure intuition of faith, theologians had difficulty reconciling with the teaching of the Scriptures and with other doctrines formally taught by the magisterium. It was only after these difficulties were overcome, and in response to the persistent petitions of the faithful, that the pope confidently proclaimed the doctrine of Mary's Immaculate Conception as a divinely revealed truth.

What was it, then, that the "simple faithful" believed, and why did some great theologians have such grave reservations about it? In the first place, they believed that the Virgin Mary was "full of grace" (Luke 1:28), for this is how the angel Gabriel addressed her (§16, 54–5). And they believed that she was sinless, in the sense that she never personally committed a sin.[6] They were confident of this on the basis of the Gospel testimony, even though some early theologians had disputed it (§38, note 8), and their confidence won the day. From apostolic times, the Virgin

6 See *CCC* §§ 411 and 493.

Mary was seen not only as the "virgin" of Isaiah's prophecy (Matthew 1:23, citing Isaiah 7:14 LXX), but also as the counterpart of "virgin Eve" (§12, 33, 36). This second association arose quite readily in the minds of Christians who contemplated the Scriptures. Picturing Mary of Nazareth at the Annunciation, they noticed that whereas Eve listened to the devil and through her disobedience brought death, Mary listened to the angel and through her obedience brought life (§35–8). Perhaps taking the cue from John's Gospel (John 2:4 and 19:26), they recognized Mary as the "woman" identified in Genesis 3:15 (§24, 26-27). In this early proclamation of the Gospel, or *protoevangelium*, God's promise included a "woman" whose "seed" would triumph over the "seed" of the ancient enemy (§28, note 4).[7] By comparing Mary with Eve, they came to understand the contribution she made as the mother of the Messiah, and the implied correspondence between her obedience and his.

Christian piety supplied Mary with a biography by means of legends recorded in a second-century work, the *Protoevangelium of James*. The legends lack the authority of the canonical Scriptures; nevertheless, they attest

7 Genesis 3:15 plays a larger role in traditional Roman Catholic reflection on Mary than it does in the ARCIC statement.

to popular belief in God's activity in the circumstances of her conception. On the basis of this belief
and the proximity of the holy sites where the events
were reputed to have taken place, Christians in the
East began to commemorate as feast days Mary's
conception, nativity, presentation in the Temple, and
dormition (§40). We can see a kind of impulse for
symmetry at work here, the Marian feasts matching
those of Our Lord. The institution of a feast of her
conception, originally called "the Conception of St
Anne" (as it still is in the East), can be traced to the
late seventh century in Syria. From the East, this feast
gradually migrated to various local churches in the
West. The feast of Mary's nativity was already on the
calendar; this addition was welcomed and initially
gave no cause for surprise. The tradition of praising
Mary as 'full of grace', 'Ever-Virgin', 'All-holy', 'spotless', and 'immaculate' had become firmly fixed not
only in popular piety but also in liturgical texts and
homiletic practice.

When misgivings about the propriety of celebrating
Mary's conception arose it was not because of any
doubt about her predestination and election in
Christ, or about her personal holiness, but because
of an apparent conflict with the Augustinian teaching on original sin and its transmission that prevailed

in the Latin West.[8] This teaching was provoked by the fifth-century heretic Pelagius who taught that infants who died without baptism could nevertheless gain eternal life. St Augustine (†430), in response to Pelagius, defended the necessity of baptism on the basis of the Lord's command (John 3:5) and St Paul's assertion that all human beings have sinned "in Adam" (Romans 5:12), and are redeemed by Christ the one Mediator (1 Timothy 2:4). Even infants who cannot have committed personal sin are brought to the baptismal font to be exorcised, exsufflated, and washed clean. Even tiny infants are in need of Christ as their Saviour and are baptized for the forgiveness of sins, in their case, of original sin. Pressed to refute the Pelagian error that Adam's sin affected his descendants only because they followed his bad example, Augustine taught that original sin is passed on not by imitation but by generation. He theorised that this sin is transmitted from parent to child in the act of procreation. Augustine evidently saw the possible implications of this for Mary's case, but avoided drawing any specific conclusions (§38).

This teaching posed a problem for theologians in the West on two counts. They had acclaimed the Virgin

8 See John Meyendorff, *Byzantine Theology* (New York: Fordham University Press, 1974), 147ff., for the tradition in the East.

Mary as holy and perfectly sinless, quite independently of these reflections on original sin and its transmission. Since she was conceived by her parents in the usual way, however, they felt obliged to assume that she had contracted original sin. Theologians differed over when her sanctification took place — while she carried her Saviour in her womb, at the Annunciation, at her birth, or even while she was still in her own mother's womb (like St John the Baptist) – but they all assumed that she was "conceived in sin" (Psalm 50:1). St Anselm of Canterbury (†1109), a great champion of Mary's purity and holiness, advanced the doctrine significantly when he reasoned that original sin need not entail active concupiscence but may be understood simply as the absence of justice (or sanctifying grace); still, he could not think how Our Lady might have escaped this contagion from her parents. His fellow monk, Eadmer (†c.1128), in a treatise on Mary's Conception, defended the feast on the grounds that God could certainly have preserved her from this contagion, and that simple people believed that he had. St Bernard of Clairvaux (†1153), however, for all his ardent devotion to Mary, objected to the celebration of the feast because he could not reconcile it with the teaching on original sin.

By the Middle Ages it was generally accepted that Mary was sanctified before her birth. The dispute that took place, then, was about the 'timing' of her sanctification (§42). For the 'Angelic Doctor', St Thomas Aquinas (†1274), the obstacle lay not in the circumstances of her conception (he rejected Augustine's hypothesis that its transmission was due to the concupiscence involved in sexual intercourse), but in the problem Mary's 'exemption' from the inheritance of Adam's sin would pose to the office of Christ as the universal Mediator of salvation. If Christ is the universal redeemer, which he is, all human beings must need to be redeemed. For Mary to be included among those redeemed by Christ, she must have incurred original sin before she was sanctified.[9] The English Franciscan, Blessed John Duns Scotus (†1308), disagreed. By a process of reasoning that earned him the epithet the 'Subtle Doctor', he proposed that the merits of Christ were applied to Mary in a unique way, 'preserving' her from original sin rather than 'freeing' her from it after it was contracted. According to Scotus, Christ's mediation of the grace of salvation was not excluded, but was exercised most perfectly in her

9 See *Summa Theologicae* III, Q. 27, a. 2; see also *STh* I-II, Q. 81, a. 3.

regard.[10] Mary was perfectly redeemed; at the moment of her conception, she was preserved, by the anticipated merits of her Son, from the contagion of original sin.

The definition of the doctrine in terms of "freedom from all stain of original sin" rather than "fullness of grace" is due, then, to the shape this controversy took. The 'maculists' held that Mary was conceived in sin, and then delivered from it; the 'immaculists', that she was preserved from original sin from the 'first moment' of her conception. The disagreement between the two parties—"perhaps the most prolonged and passionate debate that has ever been carried on in Catholic theology" [11]—lasted for centuries. Very gradually, under the guidance of the papal magisterium, the objections of the 'maculist' theologians were met. The papal definition is based on the *sensus fidelium*, not the argument of Duns Scotus, but clearly his ingenious solution helped to clear the way for its acceptance. By the late eighteenth and early nineteenth century, the faithful were asking the

10 See John Duns Scotus, *Four Questions on Mary,* trans. and with introduction and notes by Allan B. Wolter (St. Bonaventure, NY: Franciscan Institute, 2000).

11 Edward Dennis O'Connor, *The Dogma of the Immaculate Conception: History and Significance* (Notre Dame, Ind.: University of Notre Dame Press, 1958), vi.

Pope to define Mary's 'Immaculate Conception' as a truth of the faith (§47). After intensive study and formal consultation with the bishops of the Catholic Church regarding the faith of their people, Pope Pius IX proceeded to do just that.

The definition is found in *Ineffabilis Deus*, a Papal Bull issued in 1854. The terms of the definition are precise:

We declare, pronounce, and define: the doctrine which holds that the most Blessed Virgin Mary was, from the first moment of her conception, by a singular grace and privilege of almighty God and in view of the merits of Christ Jesus the Saviour of the human race, preserved immune from all stain of original sin, is revealed by God and, therefore, firmly and constantly to be believed by all the faithful.

The *object* of Mary's privilege is that she is preserved "immune from all stain of *original sin*". Catholic teaching on original sin, considered as the inheritance of fallen humanity, was formulated in a decree of the Council of Trent and is summarized in the *Catechism of the Catholic Church*. It is "a deprivation of original holiness and justice" which leaves human nature wounded in its natural powers and inclined to sin.[12] The expression "*all stain* of original sin" had been in common use since the composition of liturgical texts in the fifteenth century; it refers simply to "all that is truly sin", and does not imply Mary's immunity from concupiscence.[13]

The *subject* of the privilege is the *Blessed Virgin Mary* herself, from the first moment of her conception. Up until shortly before the definition, the draft-text identified the subject as Mary's soul, but the Pope changed the final text in order to eliminate reference to scholastic distinctions and disputes (§42). The subject is Mary herself *from the first moment of her conception.* Again, the history of the text's composition indicates that the Pope deliberately steered clear of scholastic distinctions (e.g., the creation of her soul and its infusion into her body; active, passive, and consummated conception), choosing to say only that Mary was preserved from all stain of original sin from the *first moment* of her personal existence. This finalises the judgement, already pronounced by Pope Alexander VII in 1661, that what the Church honours is not a 'sanctification' which would have taken place in the *second* moment of Mary's existence, but her 'Immaculate Conception'.

12 See *CCC* §403–9, at 405.
13 See Pope John Paul II, 'Pius IX Defined the Immaculate Conception', *Audience* of June 12, 1996.

As to the *mode by which this was accomplished*, the Blessed Virgin was "preserved by a singular grace and privilege of Almighty God, in view of the merits of Christ Jesus, Saviour of the human race". This very careful formulation addresses each of the disputed questions. The word *preserved* is used in its proper sense, that is, the definition does not say that Mary was exempt from original sin, or that she simply failed to contract it. Rather, she was "preserved" from it. Her preservation, then, was a mode of redemption: the Bull says elsewhere that Mary "was *redeemed* in a manner more sublime".[14] *By a singular grace and privilege* refers to the fact that Mary alone was redeemed in this way; she alone was "preserved" rather than "freed" from original sin. And this grace was given her "*in view of the merits of Christ Jesus the Saviour of the human race*". The merits of Christ, in other words, have a causal influence here. Just as he is the "meritorious cause" of our justification (as the Council of Trent teaches),[15] so it is in view of his foreseen merits that Mary is preserved from original sin. That Mary was redeemed by Christ follows from the definition as a conclusion.

14 *Ineffabilis Deus*. 8. The Second Vatican Council quotes this in *Lumen Gentium* 53.
15 Decree on Justification, Sess. VI, ch. 7 (DS 1529).

THE GLORIOUS ASSUMPTION

The dogma of the Virgin Mary's Assumption confirms and confesses the Church's faith that Our Lord shared with his Mother the fullness of his victory over death, bringing her with him to glory when her life had ended. The New Testament says nothing directly about Mary's Assumption, nor is there even a reliable tradition about how her life came to an end, so we cannot appeal to history for facts. The apocryphal accounts—the *Transitus Mariae* narratives —that arose centuries after her death or 'dormition' have no historical value (§40).[16] Pope Pius XII deliberately omitted any reference to them in *Munificentissimus Deus*. Neither did he attempt to prove by historical data that this mystery belongs to the apostolic teaching. His conviction regarding its place in the deposit of faith is based on the present faith of the Church as expressed in doctrine and devotion (in this case, in the liturgical celebration of the Assumption and its commemoration in the Rosary). He takes the fact that the whole Church believes that God has taken Mary to heavenly glory, body and soul, as an expression of the *sensus fidelium*.

16 The story of the Dormition was told "perhaps as early as the late fourth century", according to Brian E. Daley, *On the Dormition of* Mary: *Early Patristic Homilies* (Crestwood, NY: St Vladimir's Seminary Press, 1998), 12.

The doctrine is not, then, rooted in an "historical tradition of an historical fact"[17] (although what God did in history is factual, not mythological); rather, like belief in Mary's Immaculate Conception, it grew out of theological reflection and, more surely, out of the pious insight of the faithful regarding what is "fitting" (§57). Given Mary's unique office as 'God-bearer', her perpetual virginity, and her unique holiness and Immaculate Conception, by the analogy of faith Catholic Christians conclude that she is 'perfectly redeemed', that she already enjoys in her whole person the risen life promised to those who die in the Lord.

It is worth noticing the sort of theological reflection that contributed to the development of the doctrine. John Damascene (†749), the "doctor of the Assumption", puts it this way: "It is fitting that she, who had kept her virginity intact in childbirth, should keep her own body free from all corruption even after death. It was fitting that she, who had carried the Creator as a child at her breast, should dwell in the divine tabernacles …".[18] In popular piety, the stress is laid on the mother–Son relationship: the Redeemer's love for his mother should prompt him

17 Ratzinger, *Daughter Zion,* 72.
18 Cited in *Munificentissimus Deus* 21.

to bring her to heavenly glory, so that where he is she also may be (see John 14:3). The intuition is not that Mary earned this as a reward, but that her divine Son, in his loving courtesy, must have shielded her from the corruption of the grave.

Pius XII is content to give evidence that this is the belief of the Church. He gathers this evidence from the Church's liturgical celebrations, from the writings of the Fathers and the scholastic doctors, and from the scriptural types and motifs which have traditionally been employed in homilies and liturgical texts. He cites these not to prove this doctrine, but only to illustrate its fittingness and eminent plausibility. Whereas ARCIC takes its cue from the economy of grace and hope outlined by St Paul in Romans 8:28–30 (the predestination, call, justification, and glorification of the saints, in §10, 53, 77), the Fathers of the Church found the promise of Mary's glorification insinuated in such Old Testament types as the Ark of the Covenant[19] (constructed of "incorruptible wood"), the royal bride of Psalm 45, and the "bride" of the Canticle of Canticles.[20]

19 ARCIC acknowledges the type (§15, 54), but not in this connection.
20 See Psalm 132:8; Psalm 45:10–14ff., Cant. 3:6, 4:8, 6:9. The comparison to the Ark of the Covenant finds support as well in Revelation 11:19. For ARCIC's opinion of scriptural 'types', see §7, note 1.

Pope Pius XII confines the definition proper to the following elements (§58):

> We proclaim, declare and define as a dogma revealed by God: the Immaculate Mother of God, Mary ever-Virgin, when the course of her earthly life was finished, was taken up body and soul into the glory of heaven.

The *object* of the dogma is that Mary was taken up *into heavenly glory*. In fact the original feast commemorated her dormition, or 'falling asleep', but with the passage of time the emphasis shifted to her participation in the life of glory with her Son. What is believed is that she—in the fullness of her person—was taken up into heavenly glory. The *subject* is again Mary herself—her whole self, body and soul (§58). Being 'assumed' in heavenly glory means that Mary is 'fully redeemed', the implication being that her body—the virginal body in which the Redeemer dwelt—already shares in the "incorruptibility" promised in the general resurrection (1 Corinthians 15:51-57). By referring to her office as "Mother of God" and listing her other titles—"Immaculate", and "Ever-Virgin"—Pius XII suggests why her Assumption is fitting.

The *mode of accomplishment* of this mystery is that "when the course of her earthly life was finished" Mary was *taken up*. Being "taken up" is deliberately distinguished from "ascending"; it is passive rather than active. It is implied that God is the agent. The question of Mary's death arises quite naturally when one reads the definition. Pope Pius XII decided not to specify that she died, on the grounds that some ancient witnesses were uncommitted.[21] Despite this doctrinal conservatism, it is generally taught that Mary died and was buried and was subsequently assumed into heaven. (Her death, in fact, is a central feature of the Eastern tradition, given its understanding of the consequences of Adam's sin.[22]) The warrant for this doctrine, just as in the case of the Immaculate Conception, is the *sensus fidelium* embodied in ecclesial practice. The definition itself has been explained as "simply the highest degree of canonization".[23]

ARCIC's FORMULATION

In 1982, ARCIC already pointed toward the Marian dogmas when it wrote: "We agree that she was

---

21 Epiphanius (†403) says that nothing is to be found in the Scriptures: "they will not find whether she died or did not die; they will not find whether she was buried or was not buried." He confesses that he does not know. See *Panarion* 78, 10–22, 23.

22 See Meyendorff, *Byzantine Theology*, 165.

23 Ratzinger, *Daughter Zion*, 74.

prepared by divine grace to be the mother of our Redeemer [Immaculate Conception], by whom she herself was redeemed and received into glory [Assumption]". But it explains that Anglicans do not find the doctrines of the Immaculate Conception and the Assumption "sufficiently supported by the Scriptures". ARCIC set out, therefore, to study the biblical witness. The members determined that they needed to 're-receive' the Church's belief about Mary as a whole by retracing its development, from the Scriptures to the present day. They provide an "ecumenical and ecclesial reading" of the New Testament passages concerning Our Lady (§6–30), and then review developments in the patristic era and in the subsequent history of the Church (§31–51). This review is the bridge to ARCIC's "fresh" reading which locates Mary within "the economy of hope and grace" set out in the Pauline corpus (§52–63). This keeps the whole sweep of salvation history in view as it pertains to Israel, the Church, and the Christian believer.

ARCIC does not simply retrace the route by which believers travelled the first time, but finds a new path to reflection on Mary's election and destiny. The implications of her vocation as the God-bearer as portrayed in the Gospels can be seen, in light of

Paul's teaching, to be related as well to her role as a disciple and the prototype of the Church.[24] ARCIC views Mary's vocation as one "predestined, called, justified, sanctified, and glorified" (Romans 8:30–2).[25] As the first fruits of Christ's saving work, she is already "glorified"; she shares now in the "new creation", the eschatological destiny of the Church. On the basis of the Pauline teaching about Christian hope, and in consideration of a pattern detected in other biblical figures, ARCIC affirms, the teaching that Mary was taken into God's glory "in the fullness of her person" (§56–8, note 10) is "consonant with Scripture", and that it can be understood only in light of Scripture. It is fitting that Mary, who gave the Saviour human birth, share fully in his victory. From the perspective of the "new creation" in Christ, it is also possible to think of Mary as one "elected" in Christ from the foundation of the world (Ephesians 1:3–5).[26] Read retrospectively (§52), Paul's teaching —together with the Gospel assertion that she was "filled with grace" (Luke 1:28)—provides the foundation for seeing Mary as "truly God's workmanship

---

24 Like the Second Vatican Council (*Lumen Gentium* 55–65), ARCIC favours adding this 'ecclesiotypical' perspective to the 'Christotypical' emphasis of recent centuries.

25 This is read on the feast of the Assumption.

26 This is read on the feast of the Immaculate Conception.

created in Christ Jesus for good works that God prepared beforehand" (Ephesians 2:10). ARCIC affirms that in view of her vocation, "Christ's redeeming work reached 'back' in Mary to the depths of her being and to her earliest beginnings" (§59; §53–7). She shares Christ's victory over sin and death. On the foundations of this "biblical pattern of the economy of grace and hope", then, the members of ARCIC agree that the doctrines of Mary's Immaculate Conception and Assumption "can be said to be consonant with the teaching of the Scriptures and the ancient common traditions" (§60).

MEMBERS OF THE COMMISSION

Anglican Members

The Most Revd Frank Griswold, Presiding Bishop of the Episcopal Church (USA) (*Co-Chair until 2003*)

The Most Revd Peter Carnley, Archbishop of Perth and Primate of the Anglican Church of Australia (*Co-Chair from 2003*)

The Rt Revd John Baycroft, retired Bishop of Ottawa, Canada

Dr E. Rozanne Elder, Professor of History, Western Michigan University, USA

The Revd Professor Jaci Maraschin, Professor of Theology, Ecumenical Institute, Sao Paulo, Brazil

The Revd Dr John Muddiman, University Lecturer in New Testament in the University of Oxford, Mansfield College, Oxford, UK

Rt Revd Dr Michael Nazir-Ali, Bishop of Rochester, UK

The Revd Canon Dr Nicholas Sagovsky, Canon Theologian of Westminster Abbey, London, UK

The Revd Canon Dr Charles Sherlock, Registrar and Director of Ministry Studies of the Melbourne College of Divinity, Australia

Secretary

The Revd Canon David Hamid, Director of Ecumenical Affairs and Studies, Anglican Communion Office, London, UK (*until 2002*)

The Revd Canon Gregory K. Cameron, Director of Ecumenical Affairs and Studies, Anglican Communion Office, London, UK (*from 2002*)

Archbishop of Canterbury's Observer

The Revd Canon Dr Richard Marsh, Archbishop of Canterbury's Secretary for Ecumenical Affairs, London, UK (*until 1999*)

The Revd Dr Herman Browne, Archbishop of Canterbury's Assistant Secretary for Ecumenical and Anglican Communion Affairs (*from 2000-2001*)

The Revd Canon Jonathan Gough, Archbishop of Canterbury's Secretary for Ecumenism, London, UK (*from 2002*)

Roman Catholic Members

The Rt Revd Cormac Murphy-O'Connor, Bishop of Arundel and Brighton, UK (*Co-Chair until 2000*)

The Most Revd Alexander Brunett, Archbishop of Seattle, USA (*Co-Chair from 2000*)

Sister Sara Butler, MSBT, Professor of Dogmatic Theology, St Joseph's Seminary, Yonkers, New York, USA

The Revd Dr Peter Cross, Lecturer in Systematic Theology, Catholic Theological College, Clayton, Australia

The Revd Dr Adelbert Denaux, Professor, Faculty of Theology, Catholic University, Leuven, Belgium

The Rt Revd Brian Farrell, LC, Secretary, Pontifical Council for Promoting Christian Unity, Vatican City (*from 2003*)

The Rt Revd Walter Kasper, Secretary, Pontifical Council for Promoting Christian Unity, Vatican City (*from 1999-2000*)

The Rt Revd Malcolm McMahon, OP, Bishop of Nottingham, UK (*from 2001*)

The Revd Professor Charles Morerod, OP, Dean of the Faculty of Philosophy, Pontificia Università San Tommaso d'Aquino, Rome, Italy (*from 2002*)

The Rt Revd Marc Ouellet, PSS, Secretary, Pontifical Council for Promoting Christian Unity, Vatican City (*from 2001-2002*)

The Revd Jean Tillard, OP, Professor, Dominican Faculty of Theology, Ottawa, Canada (*until 2000, deceased*)

The Revd Professor Liam Walsh, OP, Professor Emeritus, Faculty of Theology, University of Fribourg, Switzerland.

Secretary

The Revd Monsignor Timothy Galligan, Staff member, Pontifical Council for Promoting Christian Unity, Vatican City (*until 2001*)

The Revd Canon Donald Bolen, Staff member, Pontifical Council for Promoting Christian Unity, Vatican City (*from 2001*)

Consultant

Dom Emmanuel Lanne, OSB, Monastery of Chevetogne, Belgium (*from 2000*)

World Council of Churches Observer

The Revd Dr Michael Kinnamon, Dean, Lexington Theological Seminary, Kentucky, USA (*until 2001*)

Administrative Staff

Mrs Christine Codner, Anglican Communion Office, London, UK

Ms Giovanna Ramon, Pontifical Council for Promoting Christian Unity, Vatican City

About the editors

Father Donald Bolen is a Catholic priest of the Archdiocese of Regina in Saskatchewan, Canada. He is a staff member of the Vatican's Pontifical Council for Promoting Christian Unity, working with the Catholic Church's dialogues with the Anglican Communion and the World Methodist Council. He writes as the Catholic Co-Secretary of ARCIC and IARCCUM.

Canon Gregory K. Cameron is an Anglican priest of the Diocese of Monmouth in the Church in Wales. He is Deputy General Secretary of the Anglican Communion and Director of Ecumenical Affairs, and is responsible for all international bilateral dialogues of the Anglican Communion. He writes as the Anglican Co-Secretary of ARCIC and IARCCUM.

ABOUT THE CONTRIBUTORS

The Revd Dr Timothy Bradshaw is a distinguished doctrinal theologian at the University of Oxford in England. He is no stranger to ecumenical dialogue, being a member of the International Commission for Anglican—Orthodox Theological Dialogue.

Father Jared Wicks is a Jesuit who served as Professor of Fundamental and Ecumenical Theology, then as Dean of Theology, at the Gregorian University in Rome. He is currently working on research projects and teaching part-time at John Carroll University in Cleveland, Ohio, USA.

Sister Sara Butler is a member of the Missionary Servants of the Most Blessed Trinity. She is currently Professor of Dogmatic Theology of St Joseph's Seminary in the Archdiocese of New York. Sr Sara is a member of the Vatican's International Theological Commission and a long-standing member of the Anglican–Roman Catholic International Commission (ARCIC).

The Revd Canon Dr Charles Sherlock is currently the Registrar and Director of Ministry Studies for the Melbourne College of Divinity, following three decades as a theological teacher at Ridley and Trinity Colleges, Melbourne. He is Executive Secretary of the Liturgy Commission of the Anglican Church of Australia, and has been a member of the Anglican—Roman Catholic International Commission (ARCIC) since 1991.